A Steampunk's Guide to Sex
Professor Calamity, Alan Moore, Luna Celeste, & others, 2012

ISBN-13: 978-1-938660-03-0

This work is licensed under the Creative Commons
Attribution-NonCommercial-ShareAlike 3.0
Unported License. To view a copy of this license, visit
HTTP://CREATIVECOMMONS.ORG/LICENSES/BY-NC-SA/3.0/ or send a
letter to Creative Commons, 171 Second Street, Suite 300, San
Francisco, California, 94105, USA.

Tintype photography and layout by Margaret Killjoy.

Previously published in this series is
A Steampunk's Guide to the Apocalypse by Margaret Killjoy.

www.combustionbooks.org
info@combustionbooks.org

fonts used:
Persnickety HPLHS
TYPO GOTHIC HPLHS
Adobe Caslon Pro
Tw Cen
CARIMBO
Nars
Porcelain

SUSTAINABLE
FORESTRY
INITIATIVE
Certified Fiber Sourcing
www.sfiprogram.org

A STEAMPUNK'S GUIDE TO

SEX

Professor Calamity
Alan Moore
Luna Celeste
& others

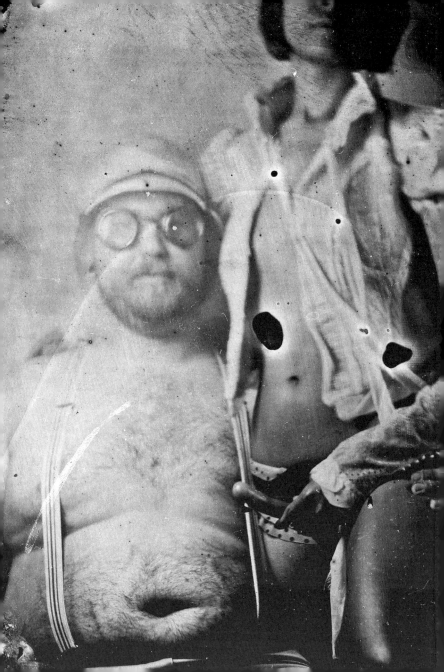

WELCOME, DEAREST READER, TO *A STEAMPUNK'S Guide to Sex*. This is a tome of apocryphal and ponderous tales of the very acts that begot our great-grandparents and it is, perhaps more usefully, a tome that describes how we might, here and now, have the most delightful sex imaginable.

Steampunk is a delightful blasphemy, is it not? Unlike simple Neo-Victorianism, steampunk grants us the license to take the history that is handed to us as holy, unmutable, and bend it to our wishes and pleasures. The same is true of sex. Healthy sex is something that is rediscovered between every couple or group that engages in it, perhaps every time. The art of it lies in learning what you want, what your partner(s) want, and acting on that knowledge uninhibited by cultural mores and socialization.

If the Victorians managed to carve out space for license and vice in their culture of sexual repression, then so too might we in ours.

Table of Contents

Introduction: Learning about sex................................5
Margaret Killjoy

CHAPTER ONE
PROPRIETY UNDER SIEGE 11

Bridal Booklets and the *Kama Sutra*........................13
Professor Calamity

Gay New York..19
Alan Moore

Venereal Disease in the 19th Century 22
Professor Calamity

Victorian Sex Slang 26
Professor Calamity

The Can-Can Dancer & the Prince of Wales...............31
Molly Crabapple

CHAPTER TWO
THE ILLUSTRATION OF VICE............35

Lost Girls & Pornography 37
Alan Moore

The Invention of Pornography 43
Professor Calamity

On the Acquisition of the Finest Texts, Visuals,
and Performances of an Erotic Nature....................50
Luna Celeste

The People vs. Lady C: Steampunks and Pornography 54
Sarah Hunter (aka "Lady Clankington")

Five Steamy Victorian Reads 57
Professor Calamity

CHAPTER THREE
ON THE LABOR OF SEX..................61

Murder & Prostitution in 19th Century London...........63
Alan Moore

Shady Ladies of the Wild West..........................69
Professor Calamity

How To Can-Can.......................................76
Professor Calamity

Becoming a Stripper 80
Luna Celeste

Steampunk & Burlesque...............................84
Talloolah Love

CHAPTER FOUR
SEX MOST PERVERSE AND JOYOUS 87

Pleasure Devices & Moral Machines. 89
Professor Calamity

Steampunk Vibrators. 97
Professor Calamity

Victorian Sexual Piercings 103
Professor Calamity

Victorian Corsetry 106
J.I. Wittstein

Make a Flogger Out of Spare Bike Tubes 112
Canis Latrans

CHAPTER FIVE
THE ART OF LOVE 117

Free Love during the Reign of Victoria 119
Professor Calamity

A Brief History of Birth Control 123
Miriam Roček

The Joys and Challenges of Enthusiastic Consent 127
Luna Celeste

An Introduction to Polyamory 131
O.M. Grey

How to Deal With, and Not Be, a Creep. 136
KC Crowell

Aphrodisiacs 140
Professor Calamity

INTRODUCTION

LEARNING ABOUT SEX

Margaret Killjoy

STEAMPUNK, IT SEEMS TO ME, IS THE COMbination of an obsession with 19th century/ Victorian aesthetics with the desire to be firmly rooted in the present. And the Victorians were, by and large, notoriously prude and not in the slightest bit progressive when it came to sex. But the thing is… these same issues are true of modern society. Erotica writers still feel the need to write under pseudonyms. Porn is consumed—quite voraciously—but actors are still shamed for it. Prostitution is illegal in most of the world. Queer sex, and even love, is illegal plenty of places. There are still laws on the books in most countries, including at the very least the US, UK, and Canada, against "obscenity," which they classify as anything—including works of fiction and illustration—that offends the morals of the times.

And the sex education most people receive is laughable. I went to public school in the US in the 90s and learned about penises and vaginas and diseases—and that's better than a lot of the abstinence-only insanity that's been going around. But I didn't learn that it's okay to be queer—or asexual for that matter. I didn't learn that monogamy and polyamory are both reasonable lifestyle choices. And maybe most importantly, I didn't learn about consent. Basically, I was in no way prepared to go out into the world and start having healthy sex. And I know with certainty that I was not alone in that.

But the repression of sexuality is an impossible task. The powers-that-be in the Victorian era tried their hardest to do so and they failed rather spectacularly. Sure, they invented anti-masturbation devices, but they also invented the vibrator. They distributed books about sex that said it was a horror that must be endured, but then Sir Richard Burton translated the *Kama Sutra*. The man who invented the motion picture camera, William Dickson, also invented the peepshow.

And it's this naughty side of Victoriana to which we steampunks owe our allegiance, I'd wager: to the rebel pornographers and dominatrices, the queers and the dandies, the mad scientists hellbent on getting themselves off. To the feminists who went to prison for distributing information on birth control. We are inspired by their courage to keep up that work.

So then, what does *A Steampunk's Guide to Sex* look like? It's a book of all the crazy things that the Victorians got up into in their bedchambers, to be sure, but more than that it's a book for the steampunk subculture. About the ways we might have sex, about all the things we can get up to.

We set our own Professor Calamity to the enviable task of unearthing the erotic strangeness of the 19th century, and he has performed admirably. He's brought us everything from recipes for Victorian aphrodisiacs to the history of genital piercings to the history of sex education itself. These pieces, scattered throughout, comprise perhaps the bulk of this book.

The history of Victorian sexuality is filled with controversy because of its very nature, and there are dozens of books published every year on the topic. It seems as much as our Victorian great-grandparents shied away from talking about "the deed," we can't get enough of poking around their boudoirs. The truth is, when the gaslights were lowered, no one really knows exactly what went on in the brothels and the bedrooms and under all of those yards of lace. Our only sources are the memoirs of perverts, the letters of passion between lovers, staged pornographic photos and films, and volumes of pornographic tales.

For the rest of our research, we looked to the steampunk community and discovered more than a few talented folks who have turned their attentions to the carnal at some point or another in their careers. We got comic book author Alan Moore to tell us what he knows about the history of pornography and gay New York, and we got him to tell us the story of prostitution and murder in 19th century London. Noted steampunk author and relationship blogger O.M. Grey has provided an introduction to polyamory. Sex worker Luna Celeste gives us a glimpse into the life of strippers and steampunk model Sarah Hunter (the notorious Lady Clankington) lets us know about porn. Talloolah Love has brought us up to date on steampunk burlesque. J.I. Wittstein and Screaming Mathilda uncover corsetry and historical undergarments. Artist Molly Crabapple tells us what inspired her to draw burlesque and what inspires her in steampunk. Miriam Roček, better known to some as Steampunk Emma Goldman, brings us the history of the fight for birth control—a fight that she and others continue to this day.

To illustrate the book, I began to shoot tintypes, using the wet-collodion photographic process to make positive images directly onto plates of aluminum. Tintypes (which were never actually shot on tin) revolutionized commercial photography in the 1850s because they were cheap, durable, and could be shot on location with the use of a darkroom built into a tent, wagon, or trunk. And believe me, the process was used to shoot a *lot* of smut back in the day.

I wish it went without saying, but I do want to make something clear. Just because you *can* do something, and just because we will show you *how* to do something, does not mean that you should do it. This book, if you'd like, will help teach you how to make whips with which to beat your partners, to manage multiple sexual and romantic relationships at once, to become a stripper, and to make vibrators out of teakettles.

But we're not telling you that you have to tight-lace your corset to be a proper steampunk. You don't have to be into BDSM or kink at all. And you know what? Despite everything society has told you again and again, it's okay to be asexual. We present you these articles on vice because we find them interesting or hope that some of you might find them useful. What does it mean to be both a steampunk and a sexual creature? This is something we intend to *explore*, but believe me, it's not something we have any interest in *defining*.

Chapter One
Propriety Under Siege

VICTORIANA

Mother-In-Law Whispers:
BRIDAL BOOKLETS AND THE KAMA SUTRA

Professor Calamity

IN SOUTHERN PART OF THE UNITED STATES IN THE 19TH century, it was tradition for the bride-to-be to lunch with her new mother-in-law—and if she wasn't blushing before she sat down to eat, she certainly was after the elder woman discreetly slid her a guide to sex, a "mother-in-law whisper." An indispensable guide to the bride's wedding night. Purchasable, in some places, directly from the wedding photographer's studio.

People in the 19th century had no small number of sex guides available to them, and all the authors of such material could be divided into roughly three categories: restrictionists, moderates, and enthusiasts. Each put out popular volumes to be given to nervous young men and women before that most climactic night of their lives.

The restrictionists' guides saw sex as degraded, something painful that was best avoided by man and woman alike. The most popular writers of these books were women—or men making do with female pseudonyms.

What exactly did these restrictionists have to say to their young adult readers? Ruth Smythers, in her popular 1894 pamphlet *Instruction and Advice for a Young Bride,* had this to say about marital sex: "One cardinal rule of marriage should never be forgotten: GIVE LITTLE, GIVE SELDOM, AND ABOVE ALL, GIVE GRUDGINGLY." William Acton, another leading light in the dark world of vice that is the bridal chamber wrote, "Quick unions are the best…. Like all chores it should be done with efficiency with an eye on completion." Other restrictionists provided an education (often quite accurate and non-sensational) about the dangers of sexually transmitted diseases and other medical ailments associated with sex, going into detail to describe urinary tract infections.

These types of guides also provided practical advice for both sexes on how to avoid lustful attention. Kimberly Kingsglover, in 1873, had these sure-fire tips for lowering the libido: men should not talk about hunting or traveling because it might excite women and should use topics like business to stop the lust building in a heaving bosom. Women could talk about charities and their relatives to calm the perverted desires of men in their company. The restrictionists had advice on perfumes, shoes, color of sheets, and even the height of the bed, all from the point of view of making sex seem sinister or unpleasant. Needless to say, virginal pain was greatly highlighted in these types of guides, causing many women and no doubt their husbands great consternation on their wedding night. These guides seemed to be most popular with the middle classes on both sides of the Atlantic and, unlike the other guides, provided few diagrams or illustrations to temper the imagination of naïve couples.

The moderates took on sex more like our high school gym teachers did as they muddled their way through public school sex ed. These guides were often mostly written by supposed health professionals and approached sex in an almost clinical style. Despite flowery names like *Truths About the Gardens of Pleasure*, they were undoubtedly cold comfort to lascivious youngsters and weren't particularly enlightening to those with little education. These types of guides came out of the reformist tradition in the late 19th century and were popular through the 1920s.

These rational guides to sex included not only glossaries of anatomical body parts and diagrams of the reproductive systems of adults, but also advice on how to sanely engage in sex. Some of these guides even advocated the use of various contraceptive devices and techniques. They also promoted hygiene as well as positions that would maximize or minimize pregnancy. They tended to be thicker than those written by restrictionists and they often had line drawings to illustrate their points. In addition to the more anatomical aspects, they did offer practical advice to young grooms and brides: "As to the clitoris, this should be simply saluted, at most, in passing, and afterwards ignored as far as possible; for the reason that it is a rudimentary male organ, and an orgasm aroused there evokes a rudimentary male magnetism in the woman, which appears to pervert the act of intercourse, with the result of sensualizing and coarsening the woman." (*The Wedding Night* by Ida Craddock.)

Dr. Blumenthal, in his 1887 pamphlet *The Veil of Love Lifted*, suggested that a new bride and groom refrain from "genital intercourse" on their wedding night and ease into it to start by sleeping together nude. Dr. Malcolm Birdsly, in his 1863 pamphlet (which was reprinted 13 times), suggested that before a night of sex both parties should refrain from alcohol, tea, and tobacco because of the adverse bodily reactions these consumables may cause which will lessen the effectiveness of the union. Other guides recommended proper washing and even stretching before lovemaking sessions. One 1896 guide had a modest 21-point preparation protocol before engaging in sex. All agreed that there was a right and wrong way to engage in physical love and proceeded through science, reasoning, and proper preparation to get young lovers ready to avoid the pitfalls of sex done wrong.

Too often, the restrictionist opinion has been misrepresented as the nineteenth-century mainstream view. In fact, many advisers wrote not about female asexuality, but instead advice to men and women on how to increase their sexual desire. The guides written by enthusiasts were often labeled as obscene and pornographic because of their positive attitude toward sexual delights and their lavish use of color illustrations. Unlike pornography, these guides sought to educate adults on how to enjoy a full and pleasing sexual experience. These guides were unique in the emphasis they gave to female sexual expression despite mostly being authored by men. The guides were heavily influenced by the Victorian vogue for all things "oriental" and esoteric—while there were enthusiast guides originally written by British or American authors, the most popular ones were translations (or fake translations) of Eastern works.

The *Kama Sutra* was probably the most well-known and popular of these sex guides from 1870 to well into the middle part of the 20th century. It was not until the late 19th century that the *Kama Sutra* again began to resume its former prominence in the textual traditions of India. This resurgence came about after the 1870s when Sir Richard Burton, the noted linguist, explorer, and Arabic translator, created a wonderful and lavishly illustrated translation. The title of the text, *Kama Sutra*, literally means "a treatise on pleasure." The 200+ pages of Burton's masterpiece are much more than a mere listing of contortionist sexual positions—the *Kama Sutra* provides a comprehensive manual of all things sexual. Although the central character of the *Kama Sutra* is the worldly man-about-town, the text was written to be read by, and provide detailed advice for, both men and women, and included pleasure-enhancing varieties of embracing, kissing, scratching, biting, use of sex aids, oral sex, and sexual intercourse. After the publishing success of Burton's *Kama Sutra*, Taoist, Tantric, Japanese, Thai, and other exotic sex guides could be found hidden on the top-shelves of private libraries all over Victorian England and America.

These guides skipped over the dire warnings against sex the restrictionists favored and also lacked the medical or scientific trappings of the moderates, and they suggested, implicitly and sometimes explicitly, the equality of the genders at least as far as giving and receiving sexual pleasure are concerned. They were the only guides a partner could go to find out about cunnilingus, for example. They contained very little advice applicable to the relations between husband and wife outside the carnal act.

These guides also tended to be expensive when compared to the cheap chapbooks of the restrictionists and moderates. Their authors tended to live flamboyant lives as explorers, military agents, foreign diplomats, and idle rich bohemians. The guides gave advice on such diverse topics as talking dirty to a lover, how to extend orgasms, how to have a romp outdoors, and the proper use of oils and tonics to enhance the lovemaking experience. Burton's *Kama Sutra* offers new lovers this piece of advice, "…those things which increase passion should be done first, and those which are only for amusement or variety should be done afterwards." W.E. Budie's guide, based on Taoist practices, offered for example the practical suggestion of using warmed oils on the inner thighs, buttocks, and the area above the pubic hair while cool ointments should be applied to balls and nipples. He goes on to suggest that scented oils should be avoided for they cover up the natural odors of lust.

We hope that this steampunk's guide to sex fits into the grand Victorian literary tradition. While it is true that this volume does not fit neatly into any of the Victorian categories (restrictionist, moderate, or enthusiast), and we do not expect mother-in-laws to be slipping a wrapped version of our book at any bridal showers, we do hope you will find in it something useful, informative, and fun to enhance your life.

Dropping Hat Pins in GAY NEW YORK

Alan Moore

In which Alan Moore describes the book Gay New York *by George Chauncy.*

I WAS RECENTLY DOING RESEARCH INTO GAY CULTURE IN early 20th century, late 19th century New York, and I read *Gay New York* by George Chauncy. In there he made the incredible statement that heterosexuality is an invention of the late 19th century. And that is true. We didn't need the concept of heterosexuality before we had a concept of homosexuality. Before K. M. Benkert in Germany first coined the word homosexuality as a form of illness. Once we got the concept of homosexuality, we needed something to define ourselves as—and the word heterosexual was coined. Before that point sexual identity was a lot more fluid. As an example, if you were a person in the lower-class or immigrant neighborhoods of New York in the very early 1900s, if you were a man going out on a night on the town, then if you had sex with another man, as long as you were the active partner, your sexual identity was not compromised at all. At least in the lower and immigrant classes, this was just acceptable behavior. It was only the middle-class element of those cities that found that state of affairs shocking, anarchic, and threatening. It was the doctors who weighed in on the debate who had the total authority, because they were doctors, and I don't have to mention that they were all also uniformly middle class and almost uniformly heterosexual. There were far fewer homosexual doctors than almost any profession, apparently, in early New York.

Gay New York is brilliant. It told me loads of stuff I was just totally unaware of, like the origins of the gay practice of referring to men by women's names, talking about them as "she" or "her," which I thought was a silly but harmless affectation. No, it's not: in early New York, gay men would often be hanging out at the automats along with all the other customers and if you were two men standing there talking… "Oh have you seen Violet lately?" "Oh yeah I saw her the other night, oh you should have seen her." People listening in on the conversation won't have a clue that you're not talking about a woman.

Loads of expressions came from that period, like the expression gay itself. Originally it was applied to women. "Gay woman" was a term that meant prostitute. And the thing is that some of the earliest, most visible homosexual men were prostitutes, so they were just called gay men to distinguish them from the gay women. Other expressions come from then too, like "she's wearing her hair up, but she sometimes drops a few hatpins." This was based upon the stereotype of gay men and gay women as "long-haired men" and "short-haired women." So if you were a gay man passing as straight, it could be said you were "wearing your hair up" but you might sometimes "drop a few hatpins" which means drop a few hints as to your true sexuality. Also, interestingly, the heterosexual phrase "to let one's hair down" comes from homosexual terminology. A long-haired man, if he was with friends, could let his hair down, and straight society just took this phrase over without actually understanding it. It's a fantastic book.

A Night with Venus, A LIFETIME WITH MERCURY: VENEREAL DISEASE IN THE 19TH CENTURY

Professor Calamity

DURING THE INDUSTRIAL REVOLUTION, POPULATIONS transitioned from rural to urban settings and prostitution became an increasingly popular means of survival for poor women and girls in the teeming urban centers of Europe and North America. This, combined with large scale conflicts like the American Civil War, led to an epidemic of venereal diseases.

Venereal diseases were not always acknowledged as being caused by sexual activity. Syphilis, for example, was considered an infectious disease that was contracted through a small wound, not unlike tetanus. While it was known to be contracted by men through prostitutes, a respectable housewife could contract the disease without her husband being accused of frequenting prostitutes.

There was a serious stigma about sexually-transmitted illnesses. Men could divorce their wives if they were even suspected of having a venereal disease—even if they received the disease from their husband. So as gonorrhea and syphilis rapidly spread, so did panic.

In 1864, responding to public pressure and sensational press accounts, the British Parliament passed the first of many Contagious Disease Acts. This law allowed local police, especially in towns with naval bases, to arrest suspected prostitutes and force them to undergo medical examinations. The "infected" prostitutes (there was no good testing method in the 19th century and thus there were undoubtedly many false positives) were sent to locked hospitals for three months or longer to undergo treatments (that did not work). Germany, France, and the US all followed Britain's lead. Of course no such laws were ever put in place for the clients of the prostitutes, thus making the laws very ineffective as ways of stopping the spread of venereal disease but serving admirably to lay the groundwork for extensive police operations of control, extortion, and stigmatization, mostly of women accused of prostitution.

In the early Victorian period there were numerous folk beliefs about how men could cure their sexually transmitted diseases by having sex with "pure girls" (children between 12–14 years of age), or with nursing new mothers, or with black women, or even by fellatio. Obviously, these "cures" only compounded the problem. Interestingly, there were no such folk cures for women infected with these diseases. In fact, gonorrhea and syphilis were considered harmless to women, despite resulting in infertility and sometimes death.

The US Civil War saw the first mass experimentation with medical treatments, as sexually transmitted diseases were threatening the war effort. The most common treatment for gonorrhea was an injection of either mercury or silver nitrate into the penis. Often this was done daily for months. Silver nitrate tablets (called mercury pills) were mass produced by the Bayer Company up until World War I. These tablets were to be taken for life and Bayer made a fortune on them. Other "treatments" included bleeding the penis by cutting its sides with a scalpel. There was also the "smoking cure" for gonorrhea, which involved a man entering a wooden box contraption that only allowed his head out. "Purifying" fumes, mostly from burnt arsenic, were pumped into the box and over the naked sufferer's body. There was also a plethora of snake oil salesmen traveling around Britain and the US promoting their cures in medical traveling shows. Many popular sodas of today have their origins in these dubious concoctions.

Prevention was advocated by many reformers and medical professionals throughout the 19th century. The first rubber condoms and "bonnets" (condoms that only fit over the head of the penis) were introduced in the US in 1855. They were often as thick as a modern bicycle tube and had a seam running up their length, so they were not very popular with men (though there were reports that some women liked the feel of them). The Comstock Laws, which made it illegal to send any "obscene, lewd, and/or lascivious" materials through the mail, including contraceptive devices and information, also made it impossible to ship or advertise the "Peter coats" and thus their use was limited. One Union captain did order twenty gross of the product and had them issued to his men.

In 1879, a German doctor and researcher named Albert Ludwig Neisser discovered the bacteria (*Neisseria gonorrhoeae*) that caused gonorrhea and promptly named it after himself. He was a reformer and an enthusiastic believer in the inoculation of diseases. He convinced the Austrian Government to round up thousands of prostitutes, who were forcibly injected (in the breast for some reason) with his serum. It is unclear what the official result of this "inoculation" was, but the serum didn't work and undoubtedly many of the prostitutes contracted gonorrhea from the shots. He was later sued by some of his victims, who won their case against him.

The first effective treatment for syphilis was an arsenic-based drug name Arsphenamine, also known as Salvarsan. The drug was discovered in 1910 and made available in 1912, but this arsenical compound came with many side effects. Good treatment for venereal diseases didn't become available until the 1940s and penicillin.

Mettle in Your Merkin:
VICTORIAN SEX SLANG

Professor Calamity

VICTORIANS, LIKE EVERYONE ELSE, CAME UP WITH AN END-less number of creative and euphemistic sayings to cover a dizzying variety of human sexual encounters and body parts. Below is a small sampling of popular Victorian sex slang taken from erotic novels (from 1840–1899) popular in both England and the US. So if you want to seduce a steampunker or talk dirty to a neo-Vic it might be good to practice using the parlance of love from the 19th century.

ARE YOU GOOD NATURED, DEAR?: prostitute proposition for services

BAWD: female pimp
That bawd has a whole stable of bobtails that make her money.

BELLS: nipples
Sally likes it when her bells are lightly pinched while making love.

BOBTAIL: prostitute
Bobtails on the Bowery will proposition anyone.

BONE ACHE: venereal disease
Dick didn't use a French Letter and now has a serious bone ache.

BLIND CUPID: anus
Oscar likes to kiss his girl's blind cupid.

BUBBIES: breasts
Alice prefers a plunging neckline so she can show off her bubbies.

BUNTER: street walker
To feed her family after her husband was mangled at the factory, poor Alice became a bunter.

BURNER: the clap, gonorrhea
I heard Felix got a burner but is too embarrassed to see a doctor for medication.

CAT HEADS: breasts
During sex Alice's cat heads are very sensitive.

CLASP: handjob
All Oscar could afford from his rent boy was clasp.

CLEAVER: forward woman
Alice never knots her corset—she is a real cleaver.

COCK ALLEY/LANE: vagina
Felix knows foreplay is good way to get cock alley ready for intimacy.

COOLER: buttocks
Everyone says Alice has a fine cooler.

CRINKUM-CRANKUM: vagina
In those postcards you can see everything, even the ol' crinkum-crankum.

DAB: to have quick sex
Felix and Alice had a dab during the intermission at the opera.

DICKY: woman's under-petticoat
If she lifts her dicky you should be ready.

FRENCH LETTER: condom
If you are going carousing, make sure you stop at the chemists and get some French Letters.

FRIG: sex between two women
I could hear Sally and Alice frig next door.

GAMAHUCHING: performing cunnilingus
Alice really enjoys Felix gamahuching on her.

HAVING A BUTTERED BUN: having sex after someone else.
Felix has no interest in having a buttered bun.

HOGMAGUNDY: sex
I heard Felix and Alice did the hogmagundy in the back of a carriage.

KNAPPED: pregnant out of wedlock
I heard Alice got herself knapped last summer.

LACED MUTTON: brothel hooker
Madam Alice's house has the cleanest laced muttons.

MANDRAKE: male homosexual
Oscar hung out a bar known for its good-looking mandrakes.

MERKIN: pubic wig
Some prostitutes wear a merkin to hide signs of disease.

METHODIST: male homosexual
Oscar is a Methodist but he keeps it quiet.

NANCY: buttocks
Felix's trousers accentuate his nancy nicely.

NIGHT-DOODLE: blow job
Alice gave a night-doodle to Felix for his birthday.

PLUG: penis
I don't know why Oscar is always bragging about his plug.

PRIGGING: having sex
Felix has not been prigging anyone else since he started dating Alice.

ROGER: have anal sex
Alice is pretty kinky and likes to roger.

TAIL: young male prostitute
Oscar knew many of the local tails that hung around the Bowery.

TALLYWAGS: testicles
Felix's tight trousers make his tallywags uncomfortable.

THOMAS: erection
Sometimes Oscar has trouble keeping his Thomas when he drinks.

TOFFER: posh prostitute
You better save up if you are going to proposition Lady Alice… I hear she's a toffer.

TOM: lesbian
I think that woman bartender might be a Tom.

UNRIGGED: naked
The dancers at McGurk's were completely unrigged.

VENUS'S CURSE: venereal disease
I got some medications for my Venus's Curse that I got from that redhead.

WHISPERS: pubic hair
Felix is worried he might have crabs in his whispers.

The Can-Can Dancer
& THE PRINCE OF WALES

Molly Crabapple

ONE DAY IN THE 1890S, LA GOULUE, THE STAR CAN-CAN
dancer of the Moulin Rouge, kicked the hat off the Prince of
Wales.

In one flick of the toe, La Goulue summed up the demi-
monde, and all its class inversion. La Goulue grew up washing laundry. She stole customers' drinks. She embroidered a
heart on her underwear's ass. She danced like an athlete at a
time when respectable women caged themselves tits to knees
in corsets. She was arrogant, business sharp, and sexy as hell.
She *was* showbiz.

Sitting across from her, hatless, was the future king of
England.

For one moment, you knew exactly who was superior.

That's how David Sweetman tells it in *Explosive Acts,* his
triple biography of Oscar Wilde, Toulouse Lautrec, and Felix
Feneon. *Explosive Acts* tries to prove that Toulouse Lautrec,

mascot of bohemian excess, was a secret anarchist. His Moulin Rouge posters, according to Sweetman, were more than sexy fun. They showed all the exhaustion, the injustice, the climbing behind those frilly petticoats. They were insurrection.

Was Lautrec an anarchist? Probably not. But the idea attached hard to my then-18-year-old brain. I'd had a long-standing Moulin Rouge fetish, starting with shoebox dioramas in middle school, and leading to my time as a poster artist for the New York burlesque scene. I saw myself as a latter day, female, two-inches-taller version of Lautrec. I'd curl in the corner of some swank club, absinthe in one hand, sketchbook in another, and with my talent, bribe the pretty people into liking me. When I read *Explosive Acts*, I realized I could use my art to cause trouble too.

Steampunk has a similar appeal. You get to use those brass goggles to stare hard at the dark bits of the past. This is what the best steampunk, like *The League of Extraordinary Gentleman*, does. Indian anti-imperialist fighters pilot tentacular submarines, and rape is still a punishment by misogynists for women who won't know their place.

The worst steampunk just talks about submarines with tentacles. It's like pasting a gear on an abscess. Gears are pretty. Airships are grand. But Victorian England would just have used them to kill uppity natives. If you don't acknowledge that, you make a lie.

John Leavitt wrote a short story ["The Revolutionary," published in *Steampunk Tales #3*] about an uprising in a brass-goggle factory. Think ultra-swank brass goggles, purely decorative, thousand-buck parodies of those worn by the workers themselves. That's steampunk with the punk.

What does this have to do with sex? Sex, like tech, is always the place where freedom and danger meld. For a woman of the 1870s, sex could be, if you were clever and ruthless and lucky enough, the way you escaped your lot in life. But you could have just as easily died from the pox. Sex is a historically accurate lens with which to analyze where a society frayed and broke, just as tech is an anachronistic, geeky lens. In Michel Faber's *Crimson Petal and the White*, THE novel of Victorian London, sex is social climbing, terror, disease, domination, hope, but never, unless you were at the apex of the power pyramid, simple pleasure.

Like tech, sex is used by vapid books to sugarcoat the past's horrors. See an abscess? Lace a corset over it.

Just as he did with sexy sex girls in Paris, Toulouse Lautrec points a way to do steampunk, particularly steamy steampunk, right. Gears and frills are nice. But the point is insurrection.

Chapter Two: The Illustration of Vice

PORN

Lost Girls
& PORNOGRAPHY

Alan Moore

In which Alan Moore explains the research and thought behind his and Melinda Gebbie's work of pornography, Lost Girls.

MELINDA AND I THOUGHT THAT IT WAS A BIT UNFORTUNATE that, of all the human activities that there are, sex was the only one which didn't seem to have a respectable artistic genre dedicated to it. We were trying in *Lost Girls* to redress that by taking all of the artistic and story values that you would expect to find in a work of art or literature and reapplying them to pornography. And obviously, in the course of putting our ideas on it together we had a look at a great deal of erotica and a lot of erotic fiction.

The history of pornography goes back to the neolithic or paleolithic period. We were carving things like the Venus of Willendorf back then. And yes, that may well have been a sort of fertility idol or some kind of other ritual artifact, but it was also an erotic and arousing image of a stylized figure of a woman. So it's been an impulse right since our earliest culture. In a lot of the older Greek cultures, you get the impression that images of sex were perfectly okay to have in public places, that at that point there didn't seem to be the stigma attached to sexuality that would develop in modern cultures.

In the medieval period, the main purveyors of pornography seemed to be the church. They weren't that long established and they had to compete against folk religions or pagan practices, so one of the main ways of getting people to church was the use of erotic imagery. As long as you could frame it within a kind of cautionary fable, you could have pictures of monks violating women and then sort of say "this is an example of a terrible sin that you'll go to hell for," and then it was okay. And that was very handy for the church because presenting sexual imagery in that form meant that they could have people looking at this imagery, becoming aroused, and at the same time being assured that their arousal was a sign of their impending damnation. Which I think is probably the key to a lot of western sexual attitudes. It's not in every country, but it's certainly in England and America and a lot of countries in Europe. We have ingrained this attitude that sex and guilt have to more or less be shackled together. They nearly have to be synonymous.

There are cultures where that doesn't appear to apply. In cultures like Holland, Denmark, and Spain, they have the same pornography that we have anywhere else, but they have a different social attitude in regards to it. It is accepted, it is barely even noticed, and there is not the same stigma attached to reading pornography that there is in a lot of western countries. And probably as a result of this, those three countries have far less actual sex crime than we have in England or America. They have far fewer children raped and strangled and thrown

THOMAS: erection
Sometimes Oscar has trouble keeping his Thomas when he drinks.

TOFFER: posh prostitute
You better save up if you are going to proposition Lady Alice... I hear she's a toffer.

TOM: lesbian
I think that woman bartender might be a Tom.

UNRIGGED: naked
The dancers at McGurk's were completely unrigged.

VENUS'S CURSE: venereal disease
I got some medications for my Venus's Curse that I got from that redhead.

WHISPERS: pubic hair
Felix is worried he might have crabs in his whispers.

LACED MUTTON: brothel hooker
Madam Alice's house has the cleanest laced muttons.

MANDRAKE: male homosexual
Oscar hung out a bar known for its good-looking mandrakes.

MERKIN: pubic wig
Some prostitutes wear a merkin to hide signs of disease.

METHODIST: male homosexual
Oscar is a Methodist but he keeps it quiet.

NANCY: buttocks
Felix's trousers accentuate his nancy nicely.

NIGHT-DOODLE: blow job
Alice gave a night-doodle to Felix for his birthday.

PLUG: penis
I don't know why Oscar is always bragging about his plug.

PRIGGING: having sex
Felix has not been prigging anyone else since he started dating Alice.

ROGER: have anal sex
Alice is pretty kinky and likes to roger.

TAIL: young male prostitute
Oscar knew many of the local tails that hung around the Bowery.

TALLYWAGS: testicles
Felix's tight trousers make his tallywags uncomfortable.

in canals. Which does seem to imply that by keeping the pressure cooker lid on in the way that we seem to be intent upon doing, we're actually creating a situation where there is going to be more sexual aberration.

I've often thought that it's similar to the skinner boxes. B. F. Skinner, the father of behaviorism, created little boxes with rats in them who would have a lever to press when they wanted a reward. Sometimes they'd get a reward and sometimes they'd get an electric shot as punishment. It was a way of programming the behavior of rats. In a lot of our Western societies, we are saturated with sexual stimulation every morning when we wake up to the evening when we go to sleep. It can be in the form of advertisement, in the form of song lyrics… all of our culture is permeated with sexual ideas and sexual imagery because they sell. So we're constantly in a state of low-level stimulation. Some us may be in a constant state of high-level stimulation.

Generally when people are in that kind of situation they will seek some kind of release, if only so that they can stop thinking about sex for a little longer and get back to whatever it is they were doing. Often that release will be found in the form of pornography. Now if the moment they get their release is the moment that they press that reward lever in that box, yes they get the pleasure, the reward that they were seeking, but at the same time they get the electric shock of guilt and shame. Doing that experiment with real rats, you would drive most of them mad. Doing it with human beings probably does the same thing. If the only way that you can get your sexual release is by fantasizing about something that is forbidden or is socially unacceptable then, well…

At the moment in the west there has been a lot of controversy about whether or not is okay to show even drawn images of illegal sex. It's not a problem to show images of other illegal acts, like murder, but showing illegal sex, that might be a problem. So there can be no release for certain fantasies. Even the fantasies themselves are proscribed. I think that if you were seeking release and every release came with a reinforcement of this feeling of shame and of alienation, with the feeling that you are the lowest creature in society, then why bother keeping it restrained to fantasy? As the old English proverb goes, "you might as well be hanged for a sheep as for a lamb." If you're already a vile outcast just because of your fantasies, then forcing you into an increasingly dark corner can turn some harmless form of self-entertainment into something that is really dangerous. And I think that our attitudes towards pornography tend to reinforce that situation.

So one of the things that we were hoping to do with *Lost Girls* was to create a work of pornography, which we insisted upon calling it for various reasons, that was beauty-proofed. Something that was so intelligent and beautiful that if people were going to criticize it, they would have to criticize it on the fundamental level of saying that it is wrong to show depictions of sex, that there would be no other levels upon which it could be criticized. That was the intention. We wanted to show what pornography was capable of.

Obviously in our researches we had toured quite a lot of erotic literature and illustration. I would say that probably our favorite period was the Victorian/Edwardian period. There was something about the written pornography of that period at least which occasionally seemed to be reaching towards being socially useful.

Here in Northampton, in Abington Square, there's a statue of our greatest ever local politician, Charles Bradlaugh. He was the first atheist to be allowed into parliament and only then after fierce opposition from the Tories who said that he shouldn't be allowed in if he couldn't swear on the bible. We had riots in the town square in Northampton before they'd let him into parliament. Anyway, he was the friend and probably the lover of Annie Besant, who was a leading theosophist, and was the woman who organized the London Matchgirls Strike of 1888 over here for the workers in the Bryant and May match factory who were developing what was called phossy jaw from handling phosphorous. I mean some of these girls died in the dark. And she organized the strikes. Anyhow, her and Charles Bradlaugh, they were sentenced to prison for distributing obscene literature. Now, what obscene literature consisted of was birth control advice for working-class women. That was the obscene literature.

There was no way to talk about sex at all during that period unless, by its very nature, you were dealing in obscene literature—pornography. And thus in some of the pornographic works that I read, during my exacting and rigorous research, you find that in the middle of an orgy, one of the characters would suddenly pause to deliver a monologue upon sexual etiquette, upon the importance of always respecting the lady, that she should always have her wishes respected. Which is quite advanced for Victorian times. Some stories included advice about pregnancy and how to avoid it. Not all pornographic works were like that, but some were. So it was a form of literature that people readily sought out and enjoyed reading that provided socially useful pieces of information. Which in some ways was what we were trying to duplicate with *Lost Girls*. We were trying to do a rich pornography that people would find themselves intoxicated by, but there are moral agendas in the work as well, as there used to be in Victorian pornography.

Another thing that I enjoy about Victorian pornography is that it is very different from contemporary pornography. In contemporary pornography, all of the women are conveniently bisexual and all of the men are relentlessly heterosexual. Because that's the way that modern men like it. That wasn't true in Victorian pornography. All of the characters seem to be sexually ambivalent. There was not a male heterosexual template that was being used in the same way that there is today. It was a lot more fluid. Considering what a hidebound society Victorian society actually was, in its dream life, it was a lot more of a fluid proposition. Sexual identities could flow and change.

Yellow Books, Birch Maids, and Trouser Tricks:
THE INVENTION OF PORNOGRAPHY

Professor Calamity

VICTORIAN PORNOGRAPHY

THE VERY TERM PORNOGRAPHY COMES FROM OUR STRAIGHT-laced Victorian ancestors—the term was coined in 1857 to describe writing about prostitutes. Victorian hypocrisy allowed people to write about sex, body parts, and fetishes as long as it was "anthropological" and warned about the poisonous influence of vice. So pornography was alright because it had moral content (no matter how flimsy)—what was not okay was any work that celebrated sex and kink. These were called "curias" or, more commonly, obscene. Obscenity included photos, films, and works of fiction that covered not only sex but also a host of other "degenerate" subjects like political satire, religious blasphemy, reproductive health, and criminal techniques.

While there were severe penalties—including hard labor—for creators and publishers of curias, there was no punishment in buying or pursuing these works, thus there were bookshops up and down Howell street in London and Bleeker Street in New York where any adventurous lad or lass could buy a "yellow book" or a set of naughty postcards. According to Prime Minister Gladstone, there were over 100 such shops peddling smut just on Howell Street.

Even prior to the Victorian age, there were fictional and "autobiographical" works that had loads of sex and bizarre kink in them (including some that could make a 21st century reader blush), some famous like the works of Marquis DeSade and Rabbelais, others now obscure like *The Worm in the Bud* and *The Nuns of St. Roche*.

But all of these earlier works had long philosophical treatises or moralizing in them or other non-sensual elements to them. The Europeans of the infamously sexually-repressed Victorian era were the first in the Western world to produce work simply to arouse without any other function (and often printed in English without proper spelling or punctuation since many were translations from the French). There is almost no subgenre of porn we know today that was not available to the adventurous 19th century gentleman or lady if they had enough money. As with any illicit product, pornography was expensive and was mostly collected by the upper and middle classes. The poor had to wait until the lessening of the penalties for pornography and for the invention of the cheap two-tone printing press of the late 1880s.

In 1886, halftone printing was used to reproduce photographs inexpensively for the first time. The new printing processes allowed photographic images to be reproduced easily in black and white, whereas printers were previously limited to engravings, lithographs, and line cuts for illustrations. This was the first format that allowed pornography to become a mass market phenomena, and by the early 20th century photographic porn became more affordable and more easily acquired than any previous form of smut.

STEALING A KISS:
OR, HOW VICTORIANS EVADED ANTI-VICE GOONS

Being a publisher of pornography had always been a dangerous business. Ancient Greek Salicus was stoned to death for copying "lewd" passages and distributing them on the street. In the Middle Ages, the inquisition rounded up hundreds of people who possessed or had copied curias and tortured them to death. In 1819, England passed a series of laws outlawing the authorship and publishing of obscene materials, and the US followed suit soon after. Interestingly, it remained legal to own, read, and even sell these works in bookstores. This led to a situation where there was huge, if discreet, hunger for lascivious material and a pretty shilling to be made by meeting these carnal desires.

Most authors used pen names or simply wrote as "Anonymous" and were fairly safe from prosecution, so it was among the publishers of these works where the law found most of its victims. The first was found within two months of the law's passage: in 1819, the Society for the Suppression of Vice successfully prosecuted publisher Richard Carlile for publishing, of all things, Thomas Paine's *Age of Reason*, in which he criticized Christianity and the morality of the Bible. (For this, the publisher spent two years in prison.) This proved to be one of many examples in which obscenity prosecution was used by government as a weapon to silence critics.

Unsurprisingly, many smut publishers were also political radicals.

Norton K. K. Humes, a famous London publisher who died in jail, coined the term "Stealing a Kiss" in 1837 to describe the dangerous work of publishing pornography.

So how did British and American porn procurers keep the back rooms of respectable bookstores filled with saucy titles when one could get sentenced to two decades of hard labor for having printed a flimsy pamphlet on proper condom use? Below are some of the common but ingenious ways pornographers performed their "trouser tricks" to elude the prudish authorities on both sides of the Atlantic.

GIMMICK BOOKS: Victorian pornographers often went to countries where obscene materials were not illegal (Belgium and France were the most popular) and costs for printing were cheaper. The problem was getting the books past nosey custom agents. Gimmick books were very common. "Shark Teeth" were books that had pages hidden inside innocuous uncut pages. "Ghost Books" were simply obscene books with different covers. "Pimpers" were books in which only the last paragraphs of each page were written in English—the rest, including the cover, were in a foreign language, so the reader would just read the last paragraph of each page to get the story.

SMUGGLING: Books, unlike drugs, are fairly large and difficult to hide. Diplomatic pouches, used by a variety of government officials, were a very common way to bring in small quantities of expensive pornography. The most famous case involved smuggling hundreds of copies of *The Maids of the Black Chateau* inside an Egyptian mummy.

TINIES: Nearly 40% of the 19th century pornographic materials at the British Museum (the largest collection of Victorian erotica) is made up of miniaturized books. Some volumes were so small one needed a magnify glass to read.

POSTCARDS: It's much easier to smuggle small objects, so erotic postcards became quite fashionable. Most of these were simply reproductions of photographs and sometimes had dirty limericks printed on the back. Playing cards were another common way to get indiscreet images past Victorian censors.

ADVENTURES IN PRINTING: Printing was the most dangerous part of the pornographic process. Printers were often raided and although printing obscene material was not necessarily a crime in itself (unless the printer profited directly), many printers would snitch out the publishers. To make extra money, printers would sometimes simply blackmail pornographers who had no other choice but to pay.

Printing required highly skilled labor and expensive equipment that was out of reach of most pornographers. Even if a pornographer was wealthy enough to afford a printing press, they still had to worry about the people working the press squealing them out to the authorities. To get around this, often pornographers would print in foreign countries or seek out printers in the immigrant areas (the Chinatowns in NY, SF, and London were very popular) who often did not read English. Pornographers could also purchase plates created by pressmen which were relatively cheap and then take these plates to the printers. Some printers set the plates with blindfolds so they could not identify the book if called upon by authorities. Other pornographers had parts of the book published by different printers so no printer could identify an entire work. Between 1869–71, there was a small printing house in Surrey that was run by workers who were legally blind.

There are still, in the 21st century, over a 100 countries where you can go to jail or worse for publishing or procuring pornography.

DIRTY PICTURES: With the advent of relatively cheap cameras in the mid 1800s, there was an explosion in pornographic photographs being made available to the public. Interestingly enough, many of the poses used in magazines like *Playboy* and *Hustler* were pioneered by the Victorians. Of course much of the work would be considered tame (or softcore) by today's standard, but at the time these photos offered a rare glimpse into the sexual realm.

Most of these photographs were shot in private studios made up to look like middle-class bedrooms, kitchens, or libraries. In the 1880s there was a fad for orientalism and then you saw more elaborate sets, some including live peacocks. And not content with simple two dimensional representations of naked people, the Victorians used a technique called stereoscopy (similar to the much later children's toy the viewmaster) to create three-dimensional representations of smut.

As you can imagine, it was just a short leap from 3D stereoscope images to moving pornographic representations. The honor for the first person to add movement to pornography belongs to William Kennedy Dickson, who, while working for Thomas Edison, developed the first practical celluloid film and helped design the kinetoscope, a peepshow machine showing a continuous loop of the film.

Dickson left Edison's company to produce the mutoscope, a form of hand-cranked peepshow movie machine. These machines showcased moving images via technique of a revolving drum of postcards, taken from an actual piece of film. In Britain and the US, these devices became known as "What the Butler Saw" machines, taking their name from one of the first films.

The first erotic film was the 7-minute 1899 film *Le Coucher de la Mariee*, directed by Albert Kirchner (under the name "Léar"). It was he who brought the world its first porn star, Louise Willy (this was probably the beginning of silly porn names), who starred in a number of penny-arcade short erotic films. Victorian men and sometimes women would pack cellars of bars and even tents to watch all sorts of sexual exploits on film or through private stereoscopes viewing for a penny. These stereoscopes, also called "penny-poppers" were similar to contemporary quarter-fed peepshows.

In 1895, the famous filmmaker Lumiere first projected film on a screen for an audience. Later that same year, Pirou directed a film called *Le Coucher de la Marie,* a series of vignettes about a stripper.

One of the prominent characteristics of Victorian porn films is its almost burlesque quality. That, and its skewering of family values and institutions at almost every turn.

On the Acquisition of the FINEST TEXTS, VISUALS, AND PERFORMANCES OF AN EROTIC NATURE

Luna Celeste

PORNOGRAPHY! FOR MANY, THESE LITERARY AND VISUAL REP-
resentations open up new worlds of sexual exploration, unlock
as-yet-undiscovered desires, and just simply help one "finish
the job" in haste. But apart from all that lies a conundrum for
the more frugal and forward-thinking of the lot—how might
one acquire free or affordable good-quality porn that is produced under ethical working conditions?

This begs the question—what precisely constitutes "good"
or "ethical" porn?

First, a word on how one might separate "good" porn
from "bad," aesthetics aside. From a workers' rights perspective, some criteria might include the following—fair pay, safe
and pleasant working conditions, and workers retaining some
control over the manner in which the content is produced or

distributed (or having full rights to the content thereof). From a broader social perspective, perhaps the presence of a diversity of genders and body types, opportunities for self-expression, and whether or not porn promotes safer sex practices and a culture of consensual pleasure are more important than which particular sex acts the models choose to engage in. Flagellation (referred to as "The English vice" throughout Europe during the 19th century due to its overwhelming popularity in Victorian England) might not be one's cup of tea, or one might consider bondage or bukkake downright wretched, but it's important to separate one's own subjective sexual tastes from the lived-experiences of the models themselves, as well as the objective working conditions under which they labor.

Kink.com and its affiliate sites are widely praised for their working conditions and complete transparency as far as how much models are paid (available in chart form on their website). Additionally, they encourage models to explore their own proclivities and only engage in scenes that they are enthusiastic about as well as encouraging safe words, safer-sex practices, and laying out meticulous rules and standards for the benefit of models. Sites like Crashpadseries.com and Furry Girl's sites—Furrygirl.com, EroticRed.com, and Cocksexual.com— push cultural boundaries as far as who or what's considered "sexy," and present queerness, diverse body sizes, non-gender-normativity, and ethnic diversity (as well as more "unusual" or "taboo" representations such as female body hair, menstruation, and strap-on sex), in non-fetishizing, respectful, and highly erotic ways. Blueblood.com extols the beauty and joy of subcultural aesthetic—goth, punk, and yes, steampunk— by featuring models who are a part of these scenes, many of whom possess "extreme" looks that are considered "less marketable" in the mainstream porn industry. These and similar websites generally charge a monthly fee for full access to all site content.

A more interactive option in the pursuit of online smuttiness is to make use of a webcam site. Webcam sites generally have many models (dozens, or even hundreds or thousands) who are available for private or group live-streamed companionship—chatting, masturbation, role-playing, sometimes even allowing viewers a chance to watch them have sex with a partner—usually for a per-minute fee of $1–$5. From the standpoint of a cam-worker, (this author, having been one for a time, can speak with some semblance of authority on this), the ability to choose whichever hours and however long one wants to work, to choose which sex acts fit within one's boundaries, the limitless profit-potential, and the freedom to refuse service to any customer are some of the more favorable working conditions of the profession. With an acknowledgment of bias I say: tip your cam-worker generously, as all that nail-polish and lube won't pay for itself!

How might one acquire erotic representations for free? Some of the more illicit methods (which we would never directly condone) include pirating porn via torrents and file-sharing sites as well as shoplifting the stuff in person. Less-illegal methods might include, for instance, swapping porn videos, photos, and magazines with friends; streaming free sample videos on "tube" sites; or simply typing one's sexual curiosities into the "images" category of a popular internet search engine. Free and legal online "galleries" include tons of photos and videos of a particular genre, or are searchable by genre within the whole of the gallery. And certainly the most "ethical" (and also most DIY) way to acquire free porn is to create some of one's own and share it freely with others who might also, in turn, create their own to share with you or whomever else happens along. Sex-radicals, exhibitionists, perverts, smut writers, and erotic artists interact in both on-line and real-life communities and occasionally collaborate on projects of sexual exploration and deviance, devoid of the aesthetic limitations and capitalistic profit-motive of most mainstream pornography (often created *as* a critique of this profit-motive).

However one acquires pornography of whatever predilections, it behooves one to be mindful of one's range of options, and to take some ethical considerations into account, while refraining from moralizing about the performers' choices or preferences.

The People vs. Lady C:
STEAMPUNKS AND PORNOGRAPHY

Sarah Hunter (aka "Lady Clankington")

"I WISH LADY CLANKINGTON DIDN'T EXIST."

That's not the most flattering thing to read about oneself online, is it?

To the best of my knowledge, I was the first steampunk porn model/actress/whatever. I'm not talking a little bit of cleavage; I mean Tab A, Slot B, mad science, corsets, rayguns, etc. Much of what I've filmed was commissioned for a website that, sadly, will probably never see the light of day (perhaps someday…), although there are also a few naughty photosets wandering around the internet. One such picture ended up in the interview I did for *Hustler* on the steampunk subculture, at which I felt very chuffed.

Publicly, the responses to women in steampunk have been mostly positive. Every panel or lecture I've ever done on steampunk/Victorian sexuality or "fallen women" of the Victorian era has been wildly popular. Often, many people are turned away at the door, due a lack of chairs or conference rooms not being large enough to accommodate the crowds. The attendees I speak to at conventions are absolutely desperate to see more "naughty" steampunk, whether it's pictures, toys, erotica, or straight-up hardcore pornography, which is great.

However, there seems to be a duality and hypocrisy online directed toward any woman in steampunk who dares to cross the line from being cute, coy, and slightly naughty into actually being sexy. I've personally seen knock-down, honest-to-goodness flame wars in more than one online steampunk forum in which several members said not only that they had to *protect their women* from any possibility of becoming the new "Goth girls are easy," but also that any prospective steampunk models should think twice and *consider the consequences* before even entertaining the possibility of documenting their sexy personas. Please keep in mind that I am sugar-coating the way in which these sentiments were delivered...

"I wish Lady Clankington didn't exist."

Really?

This was not directed at me, personally. In reality, I haven't a clue as to who this gentleman is. In context, the implication was that if Lady Clankington exists, as a *character*, if the *idea* of Lady Clankington exists and is *recognized* to the point of becoming a *representation* of sexual, steampunk women, then we as a subculture need to reevaluate our priorities. The implication is how *dare* we, as women, be sexual within our subculture? We are *intellectuals*! How dare we "stoop" to the level of our "baser" instincts and desires instead of holding ourselves up to our prescribed "Victorian ideals"?

I've got news for you: the Victorians were kinky as all hell. They invented the vibrator, for God's sake. Sir Richard Burton (a prominent Victorian) was the first to translate the *Kama Sutra* into English long before he was knighted for his translation of *The Arabian Nights*. When the camera was invented, guess what one of the first uses was! Pornography! They were not all the stuffy, repressed people that we've been taught to believe them to be. Don't put them on such a pedestal.

I have no objection to those who say "You know what? Porn's not really my thing." I understand that. However, part of being the "enlightened," "educated" steampunks we believe ourselves to be is to respectfully allow dissenting opinions and that means that if those people over there want to do naughty things in steampunk attire, on steampunk sets, and with steampunk props and take some pictures or make a movie of it, I'm all for it (as long as I get to watch).

Venus in Everything:
FIVE STEAMY VICTORIAN READS

Professor Calamity

THERE ARE WHOLE BOOKSHELVES WORTH OF VICTORIAN erotica out there, ranging from dirty limericks to multi-volume epics to a famous novel told from the perspective a flea (creatively titled *The Autobiography of a Flea*, by Anonymous.) Most of it is terrible (as is most erotica in general). Below are some of the best of their given type.

VENUS IN FURS (1870) BY LEOPOLD VON SACHER-MASOCH

From the Austrian weirdo that gave us the term masochism. A quirky book inside a book surrounded by a feverish dream about the goddess Venus draped in furs.

> *"To be the slave of a woman, a beautiful woman, whom I love, whom I worship!"*

THE ILLUSTRATED KAMA SUTRA: ANANGA-RANGA AND PERFUMED GARDEN (1883) BY CAPTAIN SIR RICHARD BURTON

The classic pillow book filled with poetry, humor, and bits of Eastern wisdom, not to mention athletic sexual positions. It was considered obscene by nearly everyone but was also one of the most famous smut books ever published.

"Whatever things may be done by one of the lovers to the other, the same should be returned by the other."

VENUS IN BOSTON (1849) BY GEORGE THOMPSON

George wrote a number of "real romances" throughout the 19th century that were like penny dreadfuls. This was his first and probably the first erotic novel penned in America. He was a journalist and had a fast-paced and dark style.

"…her limbs were as soft and comforting as pythons…"

LESBIA BRANDON (WRITTEN IN 1868) BY ALGERNON CHARLES SWINBURNE

Swinburne's posthumous erotic novel, richly-illustrated by Simeon Solomon, was never finished. It is very poetic and soft by modern standards but was a scandal when it came out.

"[H]e rioted in the roaring water like a young sea-beast, sprang at the throat of the waves that threw him flat, pressed up against their soft fierce bosoms and fought for their sharp embraces; grappled with them as lover with lover, flung himself upon them with limbs

*that yielded deliciously,
till the scourging of the
surf made him red from
the shoulders to the
knees, and sent him to
the shore whipped by the
sea into a single blush of
the whole skin, breath-
less and untired."*

THE OYSTER, OR THE PEARL BY ANONYMOUS

These two magazines were the *Playboy* of the Victorian times. They have been republished a number of times since. Each is filled with erotic poetry, preposterous erotic short stories, and obscene humor. None of it dates very well, but the magazines give you insight into the porn subculture of the day.

TOP FIVE STEAMY TITILLATIONS: THE BEST IN STEAMPUNK EROTICA

Talloolah Love

-1-
The Innocent's Progress, by Peter Tupper. My review for this is available from *Steampunk Chronicle*.

-2-
Unmasqued: An Erotic Novel of Phantom of the Opera, by Colette Gale.

-3-
"Mutiny on the Danika Blue," by Poe Von Page, appearing in *Carnal Machines*.

-4-
Avalon Revisited By O.M. Grey. My review for this is available from *Steampunk Chronicle*.

-5-
Love in a Time of Steam, by Elizabeth Darvill.

Chapter Three: On the Labor of Sex

SEX WORK & PERFORMANCE

Whitechapel:
MURDER & PROSTITUTION IN 19TH CENTURY LONDON

Alan Moore

In which Alan Moore describes what he knows about prostitution from his research for From Hell

WHILE I WAS WRITING *FROM HELL*, I HAD TO RESEARCH THE entire of London society during that period and especially prostitution. We're looking at a culture and a time from our own period and we do not understand the mindset of that period, so we map our own values onto it. In consequence, we misunderstand. For example, all of Jack the Ripper's victims, in all of the books that have talked about them, are described as prostitutes. Technically this is true. But to just state that starkly, out of context, gives the wrong impression. The fact is that all of the people of Whitechapel were so desperately poor that you could have had sex with *any of them* if you'd offered enough money. It means that either nobody was a prostitute in that culture or that everybody was. And it was kind of accepted.

I remember when I was growing up that there'd always been a fair prostitute population in the Boroughs in Northampton, which was the roughest area of the town. And nobody seemed to think badly of them. If anything, people felt sorry that they had to earn their living like that, although they understood why they did. I remember one of my uncles or aunts telling me a story about how my paternal grandmother one day had been without any money to buy food for the children. All she wanted was a jar of marmite, apparently, so that she could actually put something on their bread to make it into some sort of sandwich with this yeast spread. She hadn't got any money, but one of her neighbors was a prostitute, who agreed to go out and turn a trick so that she could give the money to my nan who could then feed her kids. Now, you can't really tell that story with a straight face these days. "Whores with hearts of gold." There's so much accumulated cliche, and yet, isn't that awesome? Isn't that awesome that someone would go out and have sex with a stranger to provide for their neighbor's children? I don't care if it's corny—it's astonishing.

This was how prostitutes were seen, at least from the working class. Now, I don't know what the clientele of prostitutes is, but I would imagine it would be more middle-class men than working-class men. I would imagine that to some degree, working-class women are probably more erotic to middle-class men. Hugh Grant having sex with a prostitute on Sunset Strip or wherever it was. In sexuality there is a class element, whether it's in D.H. Lawrence with his Lady Chatterly going for "a bit of rough" as we would say over here in the form of Oliver Mellors or whether it's a middle-class man going to a working-class prostitute because he finds them dirtier, more erotic, something like that. A lot of working-class men, at least back in the day, grew up with working-class women and to a degree were de-eroticized from them. Not completely, but they hadn't festishized them in the way that some middle-class men had. So there was that element. But generally in the communities in which they worked and lived, prostitutes were tolerated and even respected. It depended upon their character, it didn't really have much to do with what they did for a living. And I would imagine that this would probably have applied back in Victorian London.

Most of these women in Whitechapel made their money from all sorts of things. From selling violets, selling little bits and pieces, or if they hadn't anything to sell, they'd have sex with somebody if they could find a customer. It was for pennies. There was the famous "tupenny upright." For tuppence you could have sex with somebody in an upright position—presumably laying down cost a bit more because you'd have to find a bed somewhere. If you'd have had a shilling, you could have had anybody. Which tends to put a different light upon the term "prostitute." It was a dark and violent world, then as now—in some ways things haven't changed that much. One of the earliest suspects for the Whitechapel murders was not an individual at all, it was the old nickel mob, who were a gang of pimps basically who were running what was called a blackmail market. Blackmail back then meant pretty much what we mean by "protection" these days. And there had been some women killed before Mary Nichols, who was the first canonical victim. And they had been killed quite horribly. It didn't bear much resemblance to the later Ripper murders. It was more or less an indicator of the awful fate that awaited an awful lot of poor women around that time. This was part of the dangers that Victorian prostitutes had to face, the protection racket gangs.

Then there was the this new phenomenon erupting out of Whitechapel, as far as I know the world's first acknowledged serial killer. And the reaction to it was very, very strange. Obviously, in those months when those murders were going on, very little else was spoken of on the streets of Whitechapel. And disturbingly, some of the women in question, the women who were talking on the corners, were saying, "I bet it will be me next," with almost an air of longing. One woman said, after reading some of the obituaries that had been written for an earlier victim, "I shouldn't mind dying if people said lovely things like that about me." The thing is they were living lives of complete anonymity. Fairly cheerless lives that were probably going to be over soon anyway. I mean, most of Jack the Ripper's victims would have been dead within a couple of years, from childbirth or failed livers or something else. So for a lot of the women of Whitechapel, the idea of being murdered by this famous dark figure, being enshrined as one of his victims, having people know your name, would have almost been worth being eviscerated for. Which I think tells us something about the quality of life among the prostitute population of the East End in the 1880s.

The Jack the Ripper events were certainly an apocalypse, although oddly beneficial. Someone remarked at the time, "all of us social reformers had been banging away at this for years without any effect and then overnight some anonymous genius," those were his actual words, "some anonymous genius comes and does our work for us." And that was in effect what happened—the horror and the shock of what was happening to the prostitute population in the East End was sufficient incentive for Victorian England to take a long hard look at itself and to realize that nothing that called itself a society could tolerate this, and so they started to clean up the East End. They improved the quality of life and the life expectancy of people living and working down there. So in a way, it's the dynamics of good and evil, isn't it? That something evil happens and that leads to some good, which will probably lead to some evil at some point later along the line. And probably if Jack the Ripper hadn't come along, the life of Victorian prostitutes would have gone on pretty much unexamined. The famous publisher W.T. Stead—he was the editor of the gentleman's magazine *Pall Mall Gazette*, he died on the *Titanic*—when he was publishing in London, he once famously went to court because he had bought a child prostitute. He'd only done it to prove how easy it was to do. It was publicized in his magazine. Nevertheless, he had broken the law, so he did go to court for that.

But it's against the backdrop of 19th century London. Social commenters of the day were talking about how they'd be stepping over children having sex with one another in the streets. It was a phantasmagoric nightmare world. There were albinos being led about on chains. There were alligators wobbling through the gutters on display. There were children having sex, adults having sex with children; it was a completely unregulated world. This was probably the 1860s rather than the 1880s. Against that background, I mean, children of 12 were getting married and leaving home to set up together. It was a chaotic sexual landscape, at least by modern standards. A lot of the things we take for granted now, things like age of consent and stuff like that, didn't exist. Against that background you've got all of this odd Victorian sexuality erupting that expressed itself in terms of pornography, it terms of the incredible repression of the middle classes. I don't know whether or not they actually did put little skirts over the furniture legs because their furniture legs would have been too arousing, I don't think that was why they did it. But that *is* the general way they used to think.

I sometimes suspect that the sexual repression was deliberate, because sexual repression does lead to greater license. I mean the Victorian era, while very prim, had other expressions of sexuality other than prostitution and porn. Well, I suppose it was a form of pornography… this is something that Malcolm McLaren told me about, because he was quite an expert on Victorian porno. He was talking to me about the home playlets. A London businessman coming home in the 1870s on a Friday night, rather than popping in and picking up some adult videos, he may have gone in and bought a pornographic playlet which would have a musical score with it. And then this would either be for you and your partner or, if it was a more ambitious production, you might invite your neighbors over. And then there would be a pornographic drama acted out by the participants while one of them sat there playing the accompanying music on the piano.

So there were all of these things that were bubbling under the surface of the culture all the way through. And I do think that the public repression might have been intended to actually make the breaches of that repression more sweet, more exciting, something like that. I often thought that there is something sexual in the intentions of our censors, that in a way they're making it all dirtier. They know they are. At least that's my hypothesis.

Shady Ladies
OF THE WILD WEST

Professor Calamity

DESPITE POPULAR IMAGINATION, MOST VICTORIAN WOMEN had to work at least part of their lives just to survive. And some of those women shunned the textile mills, pub kitchens, and maid's quarters to seek out a different way to make their daily bread. Some of the most colorful characters of the roaring West were not lawmen, outlaws, soldiers, or cowboys but madams, mirror actresses, and can-can dancers. These women were called by all sorts of names: soiled doves, painted cats, high-boots, ladies of the night, skirt captains, shady ladies. They came from France, Chile, Philadelphia, and farms in the Midwest following miners, prospectors, cowboys, and gamblers. They plied their various trades in dusty plasterboard boomtowns from the Rio Grande to the Klondike. They came west on travelling medicine shows, in theater troupes and even on government-sanctioned trains to "feminize" the West.

In the Wild West, harsh puritan sanctions were not as practical as they were in America's more conservative eastern parts. And though the "proper" ladies still labeled those who didn't share their values—by virtue of dress, behavior, or sexual ethics—as disgraceful, the shady ladies of the West were generally tolerated by other women as a necessary evil. It was not uncommon for church ladies and other respectable women to have tea with the local madam in a cat-house on Sunday afternoons or catch a matinee of can-can dancing after returning from a "mirror theater" performance. Shady ladies were business women first and knew it was bad for business to entertain the husbands of these wives, thus they were very selective of whom they served. And for every mayor with a wife, there were hundreds of unattached young men who had taken Horace Greely's advice to go west to make their fortune.

Though it may seem odd, many shady women were married, some to saloon owners or brothel operators. Others were married to managers of touring variety shows. Such men not only tolerated their wive's profession but depended upon them financially. The women often operated legitimate businesses with the money they received from their more risqué enterprises.

MADAME MOUSTACHE

When Madame Moustache committed suicide by drinking morphine-laced wine, her funeral was the largest the thriving boomtown of Bodie, California, had even seen. More participants showed up for her funeral than Wyatt Earp's.

Madame Moustache was the pseudonym of Eleanor Dumont (also called Eleonore Alphonsine Dumant), a notorious gambler on the American Western Frontier during the mid-19th century. Her nickname was due to the appearance of a line of dark hair on her upper lip. It is thought that she was born in France but moved to America as a young woman, where she followed the gambling circuit out west from New Orleans. She was the first famous female cardsharp and made considerable money dealing and playing her favorite card game, the new *vingt-et-un*—known today as "21" or black-jack. With her gambling proceeds, she opened a number of brothels, or "parlors" as she preferred to call them.

These parlors followed the standards of the old West. Parlor houses, the best of which looked like respectable mansions, were often located near the saloons. To advertise the building's true intent, red lanterns were often hung under the eaves or beside the door and bold red curtains adorned the lower windows, thus giving birth to the modern term "Red Light District." Inside, there was usually a lavishly decorated parlor, hence the name "parlor house." The walls were flanked with sofas and chairs and often a piano stood in attendance for girls who might play or sing requests from customers.

In Moustache's establishments, there was always a red felt card table for those interested in a quick game of *vingt-et-un.* She also created a "pension" plan for her girls and demanded retirement after 24 months of work. She believed any longer in "the game" would harden one's heart and "no gold nugget in the world is worth the damage to the heart." Madame Moustache, like many brothel owners in the old West, allowed her girls to select whom they would entertain and the women kept all the money. Madame Moustache made what she needed to keep the place open at the card table and bar that entertained the waiting Johns.

Madame Moustache always travelled with a peacock and her hats were adorned with its feathers. She was friends with Calamity Jane and tried to nurse her from her lifelong alcoholism.

At the height of her career, Madame Mustache ran four parlors and owned half of a steamboat, but her luck ran out along with the gold rush. Eastern reforms were making their way west, many cat-houses were closed, and gambling moved away from her beloved blackjack to poker (which she always hated because of the bluffing). She tried to reclaim her fortune by borrowing money and staking it at a casino that had a 21 table. The game was crooked. She lost all the money and took her own life in 1879, at roughly 45 years of age.

KATIE "LOOKING GLASS" LOTT

The Old West had saloons and shoot-outs, but it also had stages. The proliferation of theaters and performers west of the Mississippi rivaled the West End of London and New York's Broadway. When culture reached the frontier, virtually every town, settlement, and mining camp rushed to erect theaters to attract performers. Big cities like New Orleans and San Francisco had opera houses and full theaters, but theaters in dusty boomtowns and mining camps ranged from modified stables to tents. A few were little more than platforms. Female singers, dancers, and actresses, regardless of their skills, were successful due to the fact that they were women in towns that were predominately male.

One celebrated actress was Katie Lott, the illegitimate daughter of an East Coast doctor. She quickly became the darling of the Western stage, and after being rained with money at one riveting solo performance in Dodge City, a shortage of coins was reported in the city the next day. She first came to fame by playing the *soubrette* in various travelling medicine shows and roving theater troupes. Soubrette is a term that comes from Italian operas, but in 19th century theater, a soubrette was a comedy character who was vain and girlish, mischievous, lighthearted, coquettish, and gossipy. She often displayed a flirtatious or even sexually aggressive nature. A unique style of theater called "mirror theatre" developed around these characters, in which the actress would perform solo in front of the glass-less frame of a vanity mirror looking at the audience and engaging in flirtatious acts and monologues. It was easy to stage in any environment and was very popular throughout the west.

Katie "Looking Glass" Lott was so popular she started to travel on her own with whomever happened to be her current husband (she went through at least four). Audience members could buy special tickets at her shows to win a chance to take her out to dinner. Katie pushed the envelope of what was acceptable theater and flaunted obscenity codes with her performances. Her depiction of a semi-nude Cleopatra caused a riot in Deadwood that ended with the theater being permanently closed. Katie made enough in her performances to engage in her true passion, horse-racing, through which she went on to win and lose numerous fortunes. She ended up dying in a cheap hotel in San Francisco's tenderloin with nearly $100,000 in the bank.

KLONDIKE KATE

The saloon hall dancer is perhaps one of the most enduring cultural images of the Old West. Their distinctive style crossed the Atlantic from such French venues as Moulin Rouge and the Petite Chatte. Contrary to myth, saloon dancers were seldom prostitutes, but they certainly were some of the most (literally) colorful characters in any given western town. Janette Kenny, historical novelist, described them:

"Saloon girls wore brightly colored ruffled skirts that were scandalously short for the time—mid-shin or knee-length. Under the bell-shaped skirts could be seen colorfully hued petticoats that barely reached their kid boots that were often adorned with tassels. More often than not, their arms and shoulders were bare, their bodices cut low over their bosoms, and their dresses decorated with sequins and fringe. Silk, lace, or net stockings were held up by garters, which were often gifts from their admirers. The term 'painted ladies' was coined because the 'girls' had the audacity to wear makeup and dye their hair. Many were armed with pistols or jeweled daggers concealed in their boot tops or tucked between her breasts to keep the boisterous cowboys in line."

By far the most popular dance of the time for these ladies was the French can-can due to its salacious up-skirt acrobatics. But in a way, the can-can was a self-defense training for women and more than one dancer had to protect herself by high-kicking, with hard pointy boots, some drunk patron who had wandering hands. These shady ladies made their money by taking a cut of the drinks they sold to the customers and by collecting the coins patrons threw upon the stage. Doc Holiday wrote, "A Parrot [saloon dancer] could make $50 in an evening which was more than I made all night at the card table."

Saloon girls were independent as women and often were part of "crews" that travelled from town to town together.

More often than not, they would manage their own business affairs and negotiate with saloon keepers for their percentage of the drinks. And the most famous of these saloon dancers was Klondike Kate.

Klondike Kate was born Kathleen Rockwell in 1873. She was a tomboy who dressed in boys clothing and "terrorized" her small Kansas town. Her family sent her to boarding school, which she escaped from many times and from which she was finally expelled. Her mother moved to New York, but Kate wanted something more so she took off for Alaska. She was stopped by Canadian Mounties who refused her entry without a husband, but the next day she returned in men's clothing and snuck in. She worked her way to the Yukon and became an immediate success in the gold mining towns of the region.

She combined sexuality with energetic dance performances that today would be regarded avant-garde. Her fire dance, in which she came out wearing 20 yards of cherry red fabric and began unraveling, was her signature performance.

She always travelled with a can-can crew and quickly earned a reputation as someone not to be messed with. One evening in Dawson City, one of her crew was harassed by the foreman at a local mine. After the show, Kate heard about the attack, so she gathered up the girls and they marched into the mining camp, still in their costumes, to mete out justice to the foreman. Miners gathered and started cat-calling the colorful girls and someone called Kate a whore. The girls proceeded to high-kick the miners, who fled in shame. Afterwards, Kate famously stated, "I don't mind a black eye but no one calls me a whore."

Scandal!
HOW TO CAN-CAN

Professor Calamity

CAN-CAN (WITH *CANCAN* BEING AN OLD-FASHIONED FRENCH word that sometimes meant "scandal") started off as a controversial dance that had its roots in the blue collar ballrooms of Paris. The dancers, or "High Kickers" as they were called, emerged over time and ended up in Paris at such venues as the Moulin Rouge.

The can-can developed from the gallop, a popular dance in the public dancing gardens and dance halls of Paris in the early part of the 19th century. When it first appeared in 1830, the can-can was really an exaggerated form of the gallop, with high kicks and other gestures of the arms and legs, mostly originally performed by men and only later by women.

Les Folles Jambettes described it in their article "Cancan, Allowing Women to be Naughty Since 1830!" as such:

> "It was viewed as shocking by the 'respectable' people because it implied a lack of

self-control and involved more bodily contact between participants than was thought acceptable. The women in particular were not supposed to become hopelessly out of breath, which the dance's energy inevitably produced. The can-can became a device with which to undermine Victorian values, and was part of a growing movement for change."

The can-can is one of the most energetic dances of the period, burning lots of calories and toning a variety of large muscles. It is important to be well hydrated before attempting the can-can, and pre-dancing stretch is a must, especially for the legs.

The can-can is usually danced in a line facing the audience (though some Western can-cans included reels and other formations). The line is usually made up of at least four dancers.

1. **SELECT MUSIC:** Choose upbeat music to dance the can-can. Purists would have you select a song that is in 2/4 time (also known as half-time). The tunes most associated with the dance is the gallop section of "Orpheus in the Underworld" by Offenbach, "Bad Moon Rising" by CCR, and pretty much all cha-cha music. Most can-can songs are between 5–8 minutes long.

2. **SELECT A COSTUME:** Traditional men's costumes were pretty simple with a touch of flamenco about them (puffy sleeves and bright colors) and a tight fitting vest. Women's costumes tended to be long skirts over crinoline with dark stockings and calf-high boots. Headdresses, gloves, etc. can be added. Today either gender may use any combination of costumes.

3. **CLAP AND STOMP:** As the music begins, run to the edge of the stage and start stomping and clapping in 2/4 time with the music. Once others start to clap, the "skirt raise" begins.

4. **SKIRT RAISE:** Skirt raising is one of the signature elements of the can-can, from the Moulin Rouge to the Dead-Eye Saloon. The skirt should be lifted to just below the chest with two hands and swished left and right fairly rapidly or in time with the music.

5. **ROUTINES:** Can-can tended to be highly choreographed with a half-dozen signature moves (outlined in no particular order below) repeated throughout the performance. Some steps would only be performed by some in the can-can line and others would be performed by all.

6. **HIGH-KICK:** The most signature move of the can-can is the high-kick from alternating legs. The body is kept straight and the knee is lifted as high as the chest and then fully extended quickly and brought down straight. If done quickly and smoothly creates the illusion of a much higher kick. This can be done as a line (ala Rockettes) or individually.

7. **STIRRING THE SPOON :** Draping a leg over the corresponding forearm (left leg over left forearm) and kicking out making a circle. This is usually done with the dancer making short hops on one foot in a circle. This hopping actually helps the dancer keep balance.

8. **PIGEON-WING:** This move requires some practice before attempting. It requires grabbing the bottom of the foot and extending it straight out (the leg resting along the check). Like stirring the spoon, small one-legged circular hops are used to keep balance.

9. **WHOOPS:** The whoops is started with the skirt raised high (usually over the head) and a quick spin. The dancer's bottom is thrust out and up, causing the skirt to lift. This has been traditionally accompanied by a scream of "whoops."

10. **GALLOP:** This step involves a stylized running in place, raising the knee very high above the waist and keeping the toe pointed at the floor. It should look like a prancing horse.

11. **FINALE:** The finale usually involved some sort of acrobatic stunt. The most common was a "falling splits" where a dancer would go from the pigeon-wing directly into the splits. Cartwheels were also popular finales at the Moulin Rouge. Even a simple somersault would do the trick. The key was that the acrobatics would take the dancer from the back of the stage to the front.

12. **FREESTYLE:** Steampunks can feel free to use any of the costumes or parts of them and freestyle any of the moves. The key elements of the can-can are high energy, good friends, and lots of fun.

In Consideration of
BECOMING A STRIPPER

Luna Celeste

PERHAPS YOU'VE CONSIDERED PURSUING THE OFT-MISUN-derstood path of professional erotic dance—the flexible schedule; short working-hours; high earnings; and for some, the pleasures of sensual performance and exhibitionism. But perhaps you wonder—"Where does one even begin the process, what shall I wear, in what manner will I dance, and what might my duties include?" Allow me to lay out plainly an abridged guide to the pursuit of a dancing-job, which intends to address the aforementioned queries and several others:

THE AUDITION

The quickest, and yet most stressful, aspect of stripping! Show up looking clean and well put-together: feminine, fully-shaven, combed and good-smelling, not scandalous or gaudy. Bring along a pair of platform shoes with a 5–6 inch heel, (*not* the heels you'd wear to a party, nightclub, or church), a couple of appropriate thong-panties, and one or two appropriate dresses or two-piece outfits (contact the club beforehand to inquire about dress code). You'll likely be asked to dance on stage for a song or two. Smile, breathe deeply, and dance slowly and intently, and if you feel as though you're dancing slow enough—slow down even more! Alternately, you might simply be asked to disrobe down to your heels and a thong and let the manager take a glance at your physique. Some clubs require you to participate in their "amateur night" contest as your audition. And still other clubs will take one look at you fully-clothed and give a resounding "yay" or "nay." Don't let one club's rejection whittle away your resolve—let your bravery and confidence motivate you to try other venues until you find a better fit.

BEING A DANCING-GIRL

Your earnings will depend on the timing and length of one's shift; the generosity of one's patrons; the quality of one's conversation, dancing, appearance, demeanor, and sales skills; and sometimes, pure chance. You'll likely be doing some combination of several of the following: dancing on stage(s), giving personal lap dances, selling VIP rooms within which to entertain gentlemen privately, and making commission off selling drinks/champagne.

A lap dance lasts the length of an approximately 3-minute song, during which you will seductively disrobe before the customer to at least a topless state, revealing and performing only what's appropriate within local obscenity laws and one's own personal boundaries. You may or may not reveal yourself "completely," you may or may not sit upon and grind down on the customer's lap, you may or may not touch or be touched by the customer, depending on these factors. The sort of entertainment that occurs within the VIP room varies—the standard protocol entails a mixture of lap dances and flirtatious, inebriated conversation. But this is also a site at which a customer might request more customized attention which such privacy might afford, such as for the fulfillment of fetishistic desires (foot rubs, beatings, roleplay, or perhaps dynamics of consensual domination and submission). Performing overtly sexual acts within the VIP room is strictly forbidden, or at least actively discouraged, by management and fellow dancers alike.

"Seduction" is always the key element here. Dancing slowly, smiling, eye contact, the graceful removal of garments, light touch, and the whispering of desires—from the lewd to the fanciful—into your customer's ear will arouse in them a longing so insatiable that they'll ache to spend as much time with you as their pocketbooks will allow.

An average dancing-girl pays a sum of between $10 to more than $90 to the club every shift, sometimes in addition to compensating the club between $2 and $10 for every lapdance she performs. However, this line of work is almost always profitable and usually very worth the outrageous fees and remittances.

SOME PARTING WORDS

Keep your information private. Be wary of the motives of managers, patrons, and the other workers. Don't do your patrons any favors that sacrifice your own happiness and well-being—you owe them nothing except the dances or companionship that they pay for, fair and square. You have the right to say "no" or "stop" at any time, to move their hand away from any place on your body, to walk away if they slight you, or to demand payment for services already rendered. Tip your bouncers generously, and smile at patrons who tip *you* similarly.

A hard-working dancer ought to use some of her spare time to pursue deferred passions, refine her other talents, and recover physically and mentally. This job can be stressful on the spirit and the body—particularly the limbs, back, and neck. Put down that rouge and do a few stretches, bathe in some epsom salts and fragrant oils, and take plenty of daytime strolls. Resist the allure of excessive spirits and drugs that cloud the mind and poison the organs. And remember, the glamor and novelty of this job fade quickly, so treat it as a serious endeavor and your rewards will manifest ten-fold. Good luck!

STRIP CLUBS AND POLE DANCING

Professor Calamit

Strip clubs, and their attendant shiny brass poles with curvaceous women in various states of undress, seem quite modern, but in fact working women were "greasing the pole" throughout Victoria's reign. They weren't called strippers back then, but had many different names including "burlesque dancers," "high steppers," "ding-a-lings," or simply "teases." The first of these ladies made their money dancing in the late 1830s in British music halls, the grandparent of today's strip joints and gentlemen's clubs. These burlesque shows moved across the Atlantic and to the rest of Europe in the following decades, and it was France's famous Folies Bergère club that brought the shiny brass pole to the stage for erotic dancing. Private performances, similar to today's champagne rooms, were available in a variety of old west saloons, including the Alhambra in Dodge City where both Wyatt Earp and Bat Masterson worked.

Steampunk &
BURLESQUE

Talloolah Love

FEBRUARY OF 2013 WILL MARK MY 11TH ANNIVERSARY DO-
ing burlesque professionally. It is my obsession. I have dedicated myself to nothing else for as long as I have known this
art form. It truly was love at first sight for me when I walked
in on a photo shoot for a new troupe being formed in Atlanta
back in 2002. I saw the corsets, the costumes, the hair, and the
reserved but blatant sexuality of it and I knew I needed to be
a part of it.

Steampunk came naturally to me for the same reasons, and
the Victorian era is where burlesque got its feet wet. The time
period was rampantly sexual but in a most reserved way. It
wasn't obvious—it was coy, it was teasing. Sure, the costume
of the Victorian is reserved by today's standard, but if you pay
attention to the meticulousness of details, the need for the
silhouette to be "just so," you'll see it. The ribbons of a lady's
hat were hung in such a way so as to be perfectly provocative:

brushing a shoulder or a curve demurely as if they were the fingers of a lover. An ankle might be bared for one fleeting moment, leaving the gentleman who might have caught a glimpse wondering if it were accidental or not. One begins to understand that, like a burlesque performer peeling back the layers, there's a lot more going on under the surface than meets the eye.

In 2008, I did my very first steampunk-inspired act, a clockwork doll routine done to Abney Park's "Herr Drosselmeyer's Doll" at Eccentrik Fest (run by the one and only Ms. Emmett Davenport.) I had already known I enjoyed the aesthetic of steampunk, with its flirtation and versatility, but it was there at Eccentrik Fest that I learned of the community that surrounded the genre. My love affair of the scene, its music, and its camaraderie began that weekend, and I've made it mandatory to create a new steampunk number every year or so ever since.

More often than not, steampunk finds its way into burlesque whether the performer knows it or not. Because burlesque and steampunk pull a lot of their aesthetics from the same era, it all begins to cross-pollinate. Often, a performer will do a Victorian piece only to be approached by someone after the show who says: "Did you intend to make a steampunk piece or was that a happy accident?"

I don't see a lot of intentionally steampunk burlesque acts, however, because steampunk seems to be far more of a costume culture than a performance culture at the moment. However, with artists like Pink, Justin Bieber, and Of Monsters and Men pulling pieces from the culture, I see the collective conscious merging evermore in the future.

Chapter Four:
Sex Most Perverse and Joyous

KINK

Pleasure Devices
AND MORAL MACHINES

Professor Calamity

"We men of science are called upon to pursue devices of pleasure at all costs."
—*J.K. Huysmans, Author, Decadent*

"We must bring everything we have from our progressive [scientific] arsenal to stop the war of lust that threatens our country and civilization itself."
—*Anthony Comstock, Postal Inspector, Anti-Sex Zealot*

ARTIFICIAL SEXUAL AIDS MAY HAVE BEEN AROUND SINCE THE Paleolithic, but the Victorians can take the credit for making them widely available and for setting science to the task of developing dildos, butt plugs, fake vaginas, vibrators, and the like. Being the Victorian age, with its fear of and fascination with all things sexual, most of these devices were said to be for medical uses. It wasn't until the end of the Victorian era that people began marketing some of these technologies as adding to the pleasure of various sexual acts.

At the same time steam-powered vibrators were rolling off the line in Pittsburgh, remarkably cruel anti-masturbatory contraptions were being patented at a rate of about fifteen original and horrifying designs per year. It was truly an age of pleasure devices and moral machines.

DILDOS

The etymology of the word *dildo* is unclear—the *Oxford English Dictionary* describes the word as being of "obscure origin." But some say it comes from the Canadian town of Dildo, which in the late 19th century was a sex toy boom town. The fine art of dildo carving was brought to Newfoundland by visiting Nordic housewives, who had crossed the cold Atlantic to collect their husbands from the pub. For almost a hundred years thereafter, the resourceful women of Dildo used leftover bits of old whales to create perhaps the finest recreational phalluses in the world. Whale bones were considered an especially powerful material to make sex toys out of because of the ivory of the marine mammal was considered to be an aphrodisiac. Herman Melville details this in his famous novel, *Moby Dick*.

By the mid-1800s the first rubber dildos had been invented. They had many colorful names, like widow's comforter, the little soldier, secret friend, and laughy taffy (not to be confused with the 1950s candy of the same name). Dildos could be bought at drug stores, where they were kept near the bath supplies.

WHIPS, CHAINS, CANES, AND BDSM

Professor Calamity

BDSM had been around for centuries before Queen Victoria was born, but no examination of Victorian kink would be complete without at least mentioning the "British taste." It wasn't that Victorians were the first to write about or practice all forms of sexual sado/masochism; it was just that they took to it so enthusiastically and brought their own particular flair to it. Today's BDSM scene has been shaped by these Victorian influences far more than it had been by the Marquis DeSade and Leopold Sacher-Masoch (who gave us the terms sadism and masochism). Elaborate dungeons, leather catsuits, naughty school girls, birch canes, pony-play, boot worship, and so on can be found in hundreds of photographs, films, and books of the Victorians.

Theresa Berkley was one famous Victorian dominatrix who not only invented the Berkley Horse, a device for

It was a Civil War surgeon who invented the first strap-on dildo. It is unknown what the initial medical explanation for this device was, but it was later patented in 1883 as a medical "prosthetic and aid."

There were three mechanical dildos patented in the US following the civil war. All of them were pedal-powered chair-like devices in which a person—presumably a woman—sat and pedaled, causing the dildo to be inserted. All three were listed in the medical section and no doubt were made to stem the growing epidemic of hysteria that plagued women of the time.

BUTT PLUGS

Less is known about the Victorian butt plug, but a few have survived and have become quite the collector's items. One glass butt plug, designed by F. Hermes in 1887, sold at Christies for $125,000, though most 19th century anal devices were more humble than the tulip-shaped Hermes invention. During the

Victorian Era, butt plugs in the shape of wooden eggs became popular enough to be featured in advertisements in France, America, and England. They were prescribed to "help prevent loss of sperm through wasteful ejaculation." The eggs supposedly promoted successful conception by increasing the amount of semen ejaculated. They believed that by plugging the anus, sperm loss would be alleviated.

There were also numerous mechanical devices made from steel, wood, and even stiffened leather to be used anally, supposedly to relieve constipation, but one such device had the same name, the Secret Friend, as a popular female dildo.

flagellation which can be found in any modern well-stocked dungeon, but also ran a twenty-four hour dungeon that could satisfy up to a fifty patrons at a time. She, like many others, became a minor celebrity in England, France, and to a lesser degree in America.

The first manuals on bondage and whip types were produced in the 19th century to facilitate the BDSM underground.

VIBRATORS

Vibrators are basically inefficient machines in which some of the outputted work or energy of the machine is transferred to the task of causing the unit to shake. And lucky for us steampunks, steam engines were excellent at providing these sensual inefficiencies—the first mechanical vibrator was powered by steam. Called the Manipulator, it was invented by Dr. George Taylor in 1869. It was a monstrous machine, and the boiler and turbine were housed in a separate room from where the apparatus ends were applied to patients. Since the inventor imagined it would be used under the strict guidance of a professional medical doctor, it didn't matter that it was impractical for home use.

But the Manipulator was just the first of dozens of steam-powered vibrators that were invented and used between 1869 and 1880. The 1880 Philadelphia Catalogue of Medical Arts, a well-circulating medical trade publication, listed no less than 16 different steam-powered vibrators. The largest, called the Goliath, could serve up to ten patients at a time, all in the same room.

Electric vibrators followed quickly. Vibrators in fact were the fifth household appliance to be "electrified," just a month behind the clothes iron. In 1880, a British doctor invented the first battery-operated electric vibrator—unfortunately it could only be used for 30 seconds at a time and required a full day to recharge. This was actually the first "high-tech" sex toy and is the predecessor to our modern battery-operated vibrators, dildos, and other electronic sex toys.

The first operational and commercially successful electric vibrator, called the Electrospatteur, was invented by a light-bulb designer named Wilhelm Kohn. This physician's apparatus delivered a combination of vibration and mild electrical shock and was manufactured by the Armstrong Electric Company of Indianapolis in about 1897. It weighed in at nearly 300 pounds and produced between 20–210 volts. Fortunately for the suffering masses, by 1900 there were machines small enough for doctors to take door-to-door to relieve the suffering of hysterical women and constipated men.

While it is true most of the above pleasure devices were made to be administered to women patients for medical reasons (namely for "paroxysm," also known as female hysteria), there was at least one such machine—called the Victor—developed for the gentlemen during the Victorian Age. The Victor was manufactured by Keystone Electric of Philadelphia in 1900. The left side was an inverted vibrator, or sheath, the speed of which was controlled by the lever in the middle of the mother-of-pearl console. The right side was a pneumatic attachment, which could, as it were, either blow or suck depending on the user's requirements. Like so many other Victorian sex toys, this was marketed as a medical device, though it remains unclear what malady it was designed to relieve.

ANTI-MASTURBATORY DEVICES

Since women during the Victorian era were not considered to have sexual needs or urges, there are no real chastity or anti-masturbatory contraptions designed for or widely used by the ladies. Men, on the other hand, were considered practically powerless against their "meaner urges" and there was a booming business in machines designed to keep gentlemen from playing handball on their home court. Though there were literally hundreds of these devices in manufacture at the time, they mostly fell into two broad categories: isolation and aversion.

Isolation models, like the Angle Head, were bulky contraptions of steel that could be locked onto the male genitals, allowing the wearer to urinate but not get an erection. They came in all styles and were made of all sorts of materials. Some were made of toughened boar hide and others were inscribed with inspirational Bible quotes.

Aversion models created painful sensations for those with idle hands. The Security was an ingenious model that used small interlocking gears that slowly turned as a man's erection started to grow. These gears would "tug firmly" on the pubic hair, causing pain. Others, like the Roman Collar, had teeth that would bite into the flesh of any ungodly penis that got excited. By the 1890s there were a number of electrical anti-masturbatory devices on the market that would send painful shocks to the offending organ if it were to get inappropriately aroused. These usually required carrying a heavy battery in one's trousers.

ANTI-NOCTURNAL ERECTION DEVICES

The Victorians did not only fear conscious pleasure-seeking, but also unconscious sensual urges. Perhaps even more popular than the anti-masturbatory devices were the contraptions designed to keep men from nighttime erections. Two of the most popular models were:

THE "STEPHENSON SPERMATIC TRUSS": With this contraption, first patented in 1876, the male was able to strap his penis down with metal place-holders. It stretched down, between the legs, and sometimes generated electric currents due to its zinc and copper plates.

THE "FEATHERWEIGHT NIGHT-TIME COOLING DEVICE": This late-1880s device was meant to prevent a man from getting an erection by restricting any growth. For further insurance, the device had an ingenious reserve which could be packed with ice shavings and saw dust to numb the penis so that one could have a pure sleep.

Letting Off Some Steam:
STEAMPUNK VIBRATORS

Professor Calamity

VICTORIANS DID NOT INVENT THE IDEA OF USING VIBRATION to stimulate the genitals. There is a persistent (and undoubtedly apocryphal) folktale that Cleopatra invented the first vibrator by filling an appropriately shaped gourd with angry honey bees to satisfy her queenly needs while Marc Anthony was away, and the first recorded moving technology was a hand-cranked creepy looking egg-beater type device invented in 1743 by a candle maker. It seems it could not have been used solo very effectively and required a partner (no doubt a medical professional curing a woman of hysteria). All the Victorians did was add steam and popularize this age-old concept.

Vibrators are naturally attractive to steampunks, who tend to glorify inefficient machinery, since basically all a vibrator is is an inefficient motor transferring mechanical energy to unwanted motion, much like a poorly-balanced clothes dryer. Steampunks have always found a way to celebrate and use these inefficiencies (and so had 1950s housewives, in the case of dryers).

There are three routes open to the steampunk looking to get their hands (and other parts of their body) on an appropriate vibrator.

There are at least two steampunk artisans (and no doubt others) who have modified modern vibrators to give them a steampunk feel. Eric Kranel of Minneapolis sold custom "Sirens," elaborate bronze mermaid sheaths that fit many standard vibrators, including one that had a globe timepiece in the handle. More recently, Lady Clankington has offered a number of "Little Death Rays" that combine modern battery technology with the bronze and wood stylings of such bygone eras as Sci-Fi Victoriana and Old West. Other steampunks have used various common "modding" techniques like electroplating, etching, patina, glossing, scrimshaw, and woodcarving to create unique and beautiful artifacts well-suited to livening up a quiet evening at home.

Just as some steampunks prefer mods and imagination, others seek out more authentic representations of past technology. One can go and find the 1869 patent of George Taylor's "Manipulator," a truly impressive example of late Victorian sex technology sure to steam up any session. Rachel Maines, author and technology historian, describes the Manipulator as

> "…basically a steam-powered, coal-fired vibrator … it wasn't in the same room with the patient, you know how in pictures of 19th century factories, you see all these drive trains that are leather straps? Well, that's how the power was transferred, there was a steam engine in one room with a drive train, and in the next room, at the other end of

the drive train, was this table with a vibrating sphere in the middle of it that you would lay the patient across."

For those reenactors that don't have an extra room for such a device, there is the simpler "Granville's Hammer." Joseph Mortimer Granville patented this little baby in 1881, two years before line-electricity. Again we turn to Ms. Maines to explain how it worked. Granville's Hammer was attached to a 40 pound wet cell battery (there are many DIY plans on how to build one of these batteries), and it had a simple brass and copper rotating motor that caused the whole mechanism to shimmy about due to the electricity alternating from copper to brass. The whole thing was wrapped in a calfskin leather and had little ivory "pots" for what we would probably call attachments. Attach your sloppy motor to your sloppy battery and you are ready to tickle the ivory with the Granville Hammer.

Unfortunately what few remaining Manipulators, Pulsers, Grainville Hammers, and their ilk that exist are in private collections or museums. The last Hammer sold at auction went for over $20,000 and it didn't even work any longer.

There are steampunks that didn't have the money to buy an original and would not settle for a modified modern electric vibrator, even one so beautiful as the Little Death Ray, and have thus pioneered making modern, steam-powered vibrators using DIY/Maker methods and healthy disregard for danger. These attempts range from those using simple Home Depot materials to those that make use of sophisticated tools and specialized skill sets. We have chosen two representing both ends of the spectrum for you to ogle at.

The first is a beautifully designed piece by engineering student (with a minor in Sexuality) and hacker Ani Niow. It weighs about a pound, is sleek and smooth to the touch, and is fully functional. Ms. Niow admits the machine gets uncomfortably hot with steam, but one could use compressed air to get the same vibratory effect without the possible scalding. Ani described the making process to Laughing Squid and uploaded detailed photos of the process on her Flickr site. The device itself has a milled, stainless steel shell with a brass motor structure. The motor is a Tesla turbine made from a stack of Dremel diamond cutoff wheels. This drives an off-center weight to create the vibration. The device has been tested using a pressure cooker as the steam source.

Creating something similar to Niow's amazing steam vibrator would be difficult, to be sure, but by no means impossible. The first step is building a Tesla turbine (which, interestingly, has nothing to do with electricity). A Tesla turbine is made out of a series of thin disks attached to a central rotor. Air or steam is injected into the closed turbine housing at the outer edge of the disks. It swirls around through the turbine blades and eventually exits near the rotor. This type of turbine can achieve very high rotational speeds but doesn't have a lot of torque or power, which limits their usefulness in modern machines. The high rotation and loss of energy can create beautiful vibrations throughout the entire housing of the motor. Niow used Dremel cutoff wheels on a steel axle, but nearly any type of thin blade on a low friction axis would work.

The next step is building a release for the steam (or compressed air) so the housing does not explode. Obviously, the release ought not be too close to the business end of the vibrator. One could use a return—a tube that brings the air or steam back out the way it came—or simply build a longer wand and locate the release valve significantly before the business end.

The third step is finding an appropriate connector between the housing and the air/steam inlet hose. The fourth step is to determine if you are going to use steam (crazy dangerous for a bunch of reasons) or compressed air and connect the hose to whatever device (boiler, pressure cooker, compressed air motor, compressed air canister, etc.) you're using. Lastly, you will have to adjust both the PSI (pounds per square inch) from your energy source and the thin blades on the axle to achieve the necessary vibration to sensually shake the housing and wand.

A much simpler design comes from the subculture of tentacle erotica (sometimes also known by its Japanese name *shokushu goukan*) which has been explored in Japanese pictorial books dating back at least as far as 1814. Some of today's adherents have made a simple steam-powered tentacle that vibrates and moves. It uses a teakettle, a hot water hose, and a small cage with a "pearl." The first step, perhaps the hardest, is to get a teakettle with a safety/release valve on the lid—since most American teakettles have the release valve on the spout, this can take some effort. One could drill a small hole in the lid to release pressure if a more suitable kettle cannot be found. Next one needs to connect a hot water hose, sold for hot water heaters, to the spout. Most spouts are between 1" and 2" in diameter. These should be clamped down with hose clamps, available at any hardware store. The next step is a bit tricky and needs a bit of steampunk improvisation—the tip of the hose is covered by a cage or some housing that allows a "pearl" to bounce about. The pearl could be anything from a ball bearing, a pea, or even of course a pearl. The cage then should be covered with something like thick, heat-resistant PVC or leather that is clamped or collared to the end of the hose.

The steam will make its way up the hose, causing it to move and the pearl to jump about at the tip to create a variety of sensations. The steam, unable to escape out the business end of a properly-constructed tentacle, will instead release out the valve in the top of the teakettle. Hopefully. And it's probably more safely applied externally than internally.

Victorian
SEXUAL PIERCINGS

Professor Calamity

VICTORIANS ARE PROBABLY BETTER KNOWN FOR CHASTITY devices and obsessive purity than they are for sex-enhancing body piercings of the most intimate kind, but it turns out that both nipple and penis rings in Western society date back to those naughty Vics as well. It might be that the only difference between then and now is that most of the Victorians were self-administering their piercings, aided only by short instruction booklets!

NIPPLE RINGS

In the late 1890s, the "Bosom Ring" came into fashion and was sold in expensive Parisian and London jewelry shops, usually behind the counter. These *Anneaux Du Sein* were inserted through the nipple with an included disposable needle. Women who were brave enough to pierce the "mother's cup" could purchase rings of silver and gold. Some were bejeweled—apparently tiny tear-shaped pearls were the most popular addition. If these women were feeling extra bold, they could purchase thin, finely crafted chains to hang from the rings.

We know today that piercings tend to enlarge the nipples (of both men and women) and that most people report increased sexual arousal from these rings, so it's no surprise that there are a number of stories to be found in late Victorian pornography that describe the sexual feelings produced by this accessory.

In his 1975 book *Anatomy & Destiny*, Stephen Kern points out that "The medical community was outraged by these cosmetic procedures, for they represented a rejection of traditional conceptions of the purpose of a woman's body." But other doctors believed nipple rings could actually aid breast-feeding.

> "For a long time I could not understand why I should consent to such a painful operation without sufficient reason. I soon, however came to the conclusion that many ladies are ready to bear the passing pain for the sake of love. I found that the breasts of those who wore rings were incomparably rounder and fuller developed than those who did not. My doubts were now at an end ... so I had my nipples pierced, and when the wounds were healed, I had rings inserted.... With regard to the experience of wearing these rings, I can only say that they are not in the least uncomfortable or painful. On the contrary, the slight rubbing and slipping of the rings causes in me an extremely titillating feeling, and all my

colleagues I have spoken to on this subject have confirmed my opinion."

—London socialite writing in *Vogue*, 1890

With the new century, the fad had ended.

PRINCE ALBERT PIERCING

The Prince Albert piercing is supposedly named after Prince Albert, who was the husband of Queen Victoria of England. He was reputed to have had this piercing done prior to his marriage to the queen in 1825, either to pull back his foreskin or to fit his member in his trousers. You see, like they are for today's hipsters, tight pants were all the rage in the 1820s when Beau Brummel, the "first dandy," started the craze. Because the pants were so tight, the penis needed to be held to one side or the other so as not to create an unsightly bulge.

Some have suggested that, in order to accomplish this, some men had their penis pierced to allow it to be held by a hook on the inside of the trousers—thus the other name for this piercing is the "Dressing Ring." And this, according to some piercing scholars, is why tailors ask men whether they "dress right or left." All of this might be apocryphal, as there is little direct evidence to support these stories, but no one knows for sure. What we *do* know is that there are reports of the "dressing ring" in gay French pornography dating back to the 1840s. Apparently in French it was known as the "Prince's Crown." It continued to be a part of the gay underground in large Victorian cities throughout the 19th century.

Victorian Corsetry:
SENSUALITY AND SUBMISSION

J.I. Wittstein

BEFORE I CAN WRITE ABOUT THE CORSET, I MUST FIRST RE-move certain myths regarding it. Women did not have their ribs removed to wear corsets, and the other supposed health effects of corseting have been greatly exaggerated by the limited medical knowledge of the time period. While regularly wearing a corset can weaken the back muscles over time (as the body begins to rely upon the corset itself for support), and the wearer might overheat and faint if over-exerted, a corset is generally no more dangerous to the health of the wearer than a brassiere is, provided it is not laced too tightly.

Urban legends about the corset aside, it was and still re-mains a fertile source of inspiration for sexual roleplay and erotic literature, as it is a tremendously culturally-loaded sym-bol of sexuality and femininity. Furthermore, I must give due credit to fashion historian Valerie Steele, whose extensive re-search regarding the history of women's underclothes is the

A BRIEF INTRODUCTION TO VICTORIAN UNDERGARMENTS

Screaming Mathilda

As we all know, Victorian women, and men, wore a huge amount of undergarments. The basic items of female lingerie consisted of chemise, drawers, corset, and several petticoats. While some of these pieces were used to create a fashionable silhouette, like the corset, the bustle, or the crinoline, most of these undergarments were not there to "style" the body or titillate sexual partners. Underlinens were there to protect valuable garments from the body and to protect the body from the dirt of the outside world. They were typically made of white linen so they could be bleached. Only the very rich could afford silk underwear.

Contrary to the practice today, corsets were not worn over the naked body. The corset was worn over a chemise and a pair of drawers and served to shape the silhouette—lifting the bust, flattening the stomach, and

main source of the information in this article.

In Victorian art and literature, the lacing of a corset, an activity that must be done with assistance, was a profoundly sexually-charged act. In fact it was often a metaphor for sex itself. A passage from an 1847 novel describes a woman actually teasing a young man for not knowing how to lace up a corset, as it was an indicator of his lack of sexual experience. The same novel described a lustful woman ripping the fine cord out of her corset in her over-eagerness for sex. A humorous picture from that period finds a husband perplexed at how his wife's corset is laced differently than how he originally did it that morning, indicating that she has cuckolded him.

Another highly sexualized aspect of the corset is tight-lacing, the act of lacing one's corset extremely tightly in order to reduce the waist as a form of body modification. Obviously this can have serious health effects, and it was a minority practice among Victorian women. Valerie Steele described how tight-lacing was viewed by Victorian society as being not merely the result of vanity, but rather, a sexually perverse habit akin to masturbation. No respectable woman would ever admit to such a practice. Despite this taboo, (or perhaps because of it) *The Englishwoman's Domestic Magazine* (*EDM*) printed over 150 letters from 1867 to 1874 (credited to pseudonyms) about tight-lacing, in which girls described extreme tight-lacing at the hands of stern headmistresses at boarding schools. Steele and other historians have noted the sadomasochistic overtones of the letters, which described "vices of whalebone drawn tight by the muscular arms of sturdy waiting maids." The language of the letters is rather florid, describing the discomfort of the corset as "exquisite," "delightful," "delicious," and "half-pleasure, half-pain."

It is also worth noting that *EDM* also received a great deal of letters about whipping, and there was an entire genre of letters advocating that boys and

narrowing the waist. Early Victorian corsets laced up the back until front clasps were introduced for fastening in front. Not all Victorian women had maids at their disposal to strap them into their corsets, and most women were capable of lacing up their corsets by themselves.

young men be tight-laced by strong women, indicating it was necessary for their "discipline." Lurid descriptions of beautiful but cruel mistresses and their maids lacing up a rowdy boy and making him meek and submissive abounded. There is no reliable evidence that any such "tight-lacing schools" ever existed, and Steele concludes that the letters are merely the fantasies of fetishistic readers and should be analyzed as such.

This fetish also existed among grown men. *Family Doctor*, a magazine which was ostensibly devoted to health, had many letters from men who wore corsets, often in improbable scenarios such as marrying a dominant woman who would insist that her husband wear corsets among other feminine clothes. "Forced feminization" is a fairly common fantasy among modern sexually-submissive males, and the corset adds yet another interesting layer to such sexual play. Unfortunately, it cannot be easily determined what letters are merely fetishistic fantasies and what letters indicated a transgender identity on the part of the writer, and little information can be obtained about transgender people during the Victorian era. One may conclude, however, that corsetry would have played a vital role in Victorian transgender behavior.

Ultimately, it is abundantly clear that the corset has tremendous erotic potential for steampunk-related fiction, media, and sexual roleplay. Its importance to Victorian sexuality and gender identity cannot be overstated. I urge any reader interested in corsets to take advantage of the extensive academic literature available on the subject, as this article barely scratches the surface of the information available about this remarkable and fascinating garment.

MAKE A FLOGGER OUT OF SPARE BIKE TUBES
(DEAD COWS MAKE POOR BEDFELLOWS)

Canis Latrans

Ingredients:
- Bicycle innertube
- Sharp scissors
- Warm soapy water
- Electrical tape (any color)
- Large diameter metal ring (optional)

STEP ONE: ACQUIRE INNERTUBES

For this flogger, we'll use mountain bike or other large innertubes (not tubes from a road bike!). If you don't have any handy, stop by your local bike repair shop and ask for a used one for your "art project." Alternately, tell them what it's for and see them blush. They'll usually have a bucket of used tubes or they'll let you dig through their trash. An ideal innertube has no gaping holes/rips and very few (if any) patches so you can easily cut straight lines. It should be round and have

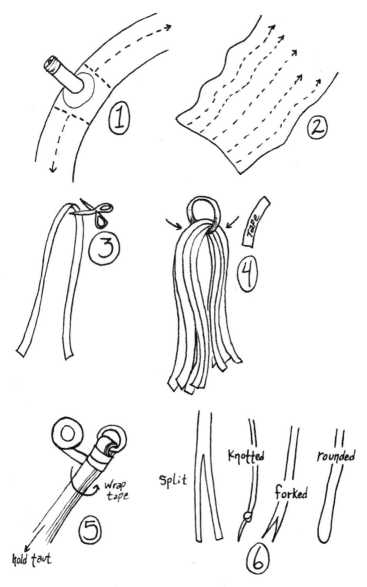

①

②

③

④ Tape

⑤ Wrap tape

hold taut

⑥ Split   Knotted   Forked   rounded

small raised lines; low-quality tubes sometimes have a rectangular profile, but are harder to use. Beware tubes filled with that green self-repairing goo—they make a big mess! Check around the valve for signs of green or white leakage, or get a few backups.

STEP TWO: PREP INNERTUBE

Cut out the valve and slice the innertube neatly down the middle (Diagram 1). Follow one of the raised lines for a straight cut. You'll end up with a long rectangle of wiggly black rubber. Your innertube probably has some whitish powder on one side (GMO corn starch) and potentially dirt/grime on the other. If there's any crusty goo on the inside, use another tube. Otherwise, using warm soapy water, wash the rubber, rinse, and hang to dry.

STEP THREE: SLICE STRIPS

Once your innertube dries, slice it into 4–7 even strips (Diagram 2). Depending on the brand of innertube you found, it will have a number of small raised lines you can follow for even strips. It's okay if they're not exactly the same width, but they should be within a centimeter of one another and as even as possible. Cut each of the resulting strips in half "hamburger" style, so you have twice as many shorter strips (Diagram 3).

STEP FOUR: MAKE THE HANDLE

Get out your tape and cut off a piece a few inches long. Fold your strips in half, although again, it doesn't need to be exact. The strips will all have a curve to them, so I like to hold up each strip until the edges are roughly even, then drape over the steel ring (Diagram 4). If you don't want to use a ring, you can leave it out and just fold the strips together. Pinch the top on the strips tightly just below the ring (or fold) and wrap your piece of tape around all of the strips. Hook the ring around something like a bedpost or your toe, or clamp it to something, to free your hands. In a pinch, sit on the ground and step on the end. Using the roll of tape, wrap over the other tape a few times, then spiral down the handle (Diagram 5). Keep the strips tightly together in a straight line or you'll end up with a curvy handle. The more tightly you hold the strips together, the more solid your handle will feel when it's done. I like to go about 15cm (6 inches) for a handle, or a little longer than the width of my hand. When you reach the end, wrap the tape around a few more times, then cut the end neatly.

At this point, you have a perfectly usable flogger with wide tails. I like to slice them in half lengthwise at least once, just up to the handle. Generally, the more tails (or strips) in a flogger, the more "thuddy" or heavy the impact. Experiment! Different amounts and shapes of tails vary the feel of the flogger (Diagram 6), although rubber will always be more "stingy" and sharp-feeling than leather. Wash your flogger between partners, and keep the rubber from cracking with a very light coating of oil (olive works well). Be careful when you use it on other people, and enjoy!

Chapter Five:
The Art of Love

SEX & EDUCATION

Queen of Hearts:
FREE LOVE DURING THE REIGN OF VICTORIA

Professor Calamity

THE VICTORIANS MAY BE RESPONSIBLE FOR A LOT OF OUR hang-ups around sex, but a number of 19th century women (and a few men) fought and dreamed of sexual liberation and short skirts. These sex radicals came together from all walks of life, both in the US and Europe, under the banner of "free love." And for those who might be confused, that is free as in "free press" not free as in "free beer."

> *"Pleasure is a right not only for men but also women."*
> —*Victoria Woodhull*

VICTORIA WOODHULL was the leading voice advocating the idea that women had the right to sexual pleasure, inside or outside of marriage. This was a radical idea in the 19th century, but Victoria was never one to shirk shaking the pillars of "decent society." She was the first woman to run a brokerage firm on Wall Street, to own a newspaper, to own a professional sports team, to own a horse-racing stable, and she was the first to run for US President. She wrote, published, and spoke out for a woman's need and right to embrace her erotic desires. She published the first article on the "feminine orgasm," based on a year-long ethnographic work she did among prostitutes and lesbians.

Her arguments for female sexual liberation were ingenious: she claimed men's own sexuality was limited by having to copulate with "lesser beings," saying only a free woman could really please a partner and herself. She also presaged Second Wave feminism in supporting a woman's right to wear what she wanted and that being a sexual being was not at odds with being a wife, mother, sister, or anything else. She most famously wore short skirts that showed off her calves and in summer months wore very short sleeves on her blouses. She argued that women's fashion should be for women and not held hostage to the lewdness of men. She wrote, "Women have been restrained, corseted, and held back for generations; perhaps it is time for our men to show some restraint so we can all be free to enjoy the bounty of our desires."

> *"The best justice is blind and so is the best love."*
> *—Fanny Wright*

Free love was not just about liberating fashion or allowing women sexual pleasure; it was also about whom one loves. **FANNY WRIGHT** was the most prominent free love rebel during the early decades of the 19th century. Fanny and her legions of followers believed individuals should have the right to love *anyone*, regardless of gender, religion, race, or class, and that no law was more powerful than true love, so they founded a free love community to encourage free sexual relationships and oppose marriage.

Wright taught that sex could be a positive experience, not just for procreation but for individual fulfillment and for the love of partners for each other. Her commune was open to runaway slaves, Native Americans, and homosexuals, who were free to love whomever they wished without sanction. Children of the community were given sex education that included the use of contraceptive sponges, herbalism, and other anti-reproductive methods. When Wright got sick and the community started to fall apart, she paid for the ex-slaves to go to Haiti (where slavery had been abolished), where they started a free love community based on Wright's ideas that lasted until 1947.

> *"Free love? As if love is anything but free!"*
> *—Emma Goldman*

EMMA GOLDMAN was—and is still—the world's most famed and notorious woman anarchist, and was considered by the US government to be the most dangerous woman of the 19th century. What is less known is that she was a tireless advocate for free love. Emma's ideas about free love were very influenced by Mary Wollstonecraft, the mother of Mary Shelley. Mary Wollstonecraft was one of the first women to contribute to the free love movement—her novels criticized the social construction of marriage and its effects on women. In her first novel, *Mary: A Fiction*, written in 1788, the heroine is forced into a loveless marriage for economic reasons. She finds love in relationships with another man and a woman. Mary makes it clear that women "had strong sexual desires and that it was degrading and immoral to pretend otherwise."

Emma Goldman believed marriage was a form of oppression and, despite having been married once, railed against it. She found the whole concept of marriage to be degrading to the power and beauty of love. She enjoyed sex with many partners and refused to be ashamed of that fact. She spoke against any laws that interfered with people and their love lives. She supported homosexuals and unmarried women, called to make divorce legal and easy, and fought for women to wear comfortable clothes. She was also a strong proponent of sex education. She wrote dozens of pamphlets and translated the works of others in various languages to spread the word about contraception and how to have a fulfilling sex life. Emma went to jail more for her free love advocacy than for her anarchist work.

These women and their ideas were not just outliers either. They were just a small part of a large free love movement that existed throughout the 19th century in the Western world, and their ideas laid the groundwork for the sexual revolutions that would occur throughout the 20th century.

HISTORY OF BIRTH CONTROL

A Brief

Miriam Roček

THE NEXT TIME YOU FIND YOURSELF SPEAKING TO THOSE WHO find artificial contraception distasteful or immoral, ask that they examine, for a moment, their history. Not their 19th century history; we must go further back than that, to ancient times when a popular form of birth control, practiced openly in societies all across the world, from India, to the Great Plains of North America, and to the cradle of Western Civilization in Greece, was cold-blooded infanticide. Morality shapes itself to necessity, and with other methods of contraception and abortion unreliable, unavailable, or unsafe, and resources limited, people quietly accepted the deaths of unwanted infants as an acceptable solution to the problem of limited resources spread between too many children.

Do not, I pray, feel morally superior because you have no intention of resorting to infanticide or infant abandonment to deal with an unwanted pregnancy. You live in a world that has many more options, and as such you have been given the privilege of being more selective. Contraception, education, and medical abortion are all that separate us from those centuries when wolves, lions, and birds of prey fed on the flesh of unwanted infants.

The 19th century saw great advances in both the effectiveness and availability of contraception, as well as (with the growing understanding of sepsis and the effective use of anesthetics) advances in the safety with which abortions could be practiced. Why, then, was it suddenly necessary for there to be a political struggle in the nineteenth and twentieth centuries (a struggle that continues today) to allow women access to birth control? The answer lies in moralism, religion, and the desire to control women's bodies.

As we all know, the culture of the 19th century English speaking world (what might be referred to as the "Victorian Era," by those who acknowledge the sovereignty of a hereditary monarch or the legitimacy of the empire over which they rule) featured a strong movement towards conservativism and prudery. The advent of birth control was thus fought largely through censorship and moralism. Rather than simply oppose birth control on moral grounds, as the Catholic Church did, (and does to this day), those in power sought to restrict access to birth control by declaring any discussion or education on the matter indecent, inappropriate, and legally "obscene." A parallel to this technique might be detectable, by an alert observer, in the current movement for "abstinence-only sex-ed" in American public schools. Ignorance is the goal, and ignorance is best achieved through a fear of, and indeed an active campaign against, information and education. Such was the logic behind the Comstock Act in the United States, which in 1873 banned not only the distribution of contraceptive devices, but the distribution of informative or educational materials on the subject of birth control, on the grounds that such materials were "obscene."

More subtle attacks on female sovereignty existed as well. The role of women was redefined, by middle-class Christian moralizers, as the "angel in the house," the domestic, self-sacrificing caregiver, a model of passivity, motherhood, and chastity. Such a woman would have no need for contraception, abortions, or any other method of preventing unwanted children; she practiced abstinence until her marriage, whereupon she would reluctantly begin having intercourse at her husband's command (any sign of pleasure on her part would, of course, have been most improper, and even unhealthy), and cheerfully carry to term, discreetly deliver, and raise a respectable number of children.

Moreover, she had no use for birth control because all forms of "control" were considered best held out of her grasp. A political voice, economic independence, and yes, sovereignty over her own body were antithetical to the "angel in the house." Her tasks were to fulfill her duty, not to choose it, and to do as was expected and demanded of her by her father, her husband, her children, and her (Protestant) church. (Note, of course, that this ideal was developed as a model for upper and middle class, English-speaking, Protestant, white women, but that women of all other groups were nevertheless judged harshly for failing to conform by the middle and upper class, English speaking, Protestant, white men who dominated society.)

Those who fought against these restrictive roles, and against the ignorance imposed by the proponents of decency faced arrest, imprisonment, and persecution. The famously fearless anarchist Emma Goldman was sent to jail for educating people about birth control, an incident that she, as was her habit, took in stride, but many advocates lives were dominated and ruined by the consequences of their commitment to birth control. Following months of imprisonment under the Comstock laws, and facing another five year sentence, sex educator and free-love advocate Ida Craddock's suicide note specifically named and condemned Anthony Comstock as bearing responsibility for her death. Lectures were broken up by police, written material was seized and destroyed—yet advocates fought on, and continue to fight the forces of ignorance to this day, because of their recognition of what the struggle is really about.

It was in this era that the term "birth control" was introduced by famous activist Margaret Sanger, demonstrating her understanding of what contraception truly meant. Prior to her coinage, the preferred term was "family limitation," but as the current term makes clear, the issue was never limitation, or families, but control—control over female bodies and lives. Though Sanger's support for eugenics make her impossible to view as a hero, her commitment to birth control and her ceaseless work to secure women's access to it make her equally impossible to dismiss.

That understanding of what contraception is really about is truly the most important thing we can learn from the struggle for birth control rights. Arguments made against contraception may be couched in concerns for morals, for decency, but these are mere excuses for their true purpose: the securing of power over female bodies. No one who would seek such power should be trusted, nor should any claim on their part to have any interest in morals or decency. Morality, as I said before, is easily bent, and as such, those who seek to control the lives and bodies of women have seized upon moral claims as a weapon. We have seen the world that ignorance and prudery created, and we have no wish to return there.

Ecstatic Engagement:
THE JOYS AND CHALLENGES OF ENTHUSIASTIC CONSENT

Luna Celeste

As the adage goes: "Consent is the presence of a 'yes,' not the absence of a 'no.'" In a culture rife with gendered double-standards, shaming of certain types of bodies or desires, a de-emphasis on healthy communication, and some highly-problematic ideas with regards to sexual entitlement over other people's bodies (particularly the bodies of those not identified as "male"), it's no wonder why conveying a genuine, emphatic "yes" or "no" can be particularly trying! We are taught, implicitly or explicitly, that silence constitutes consent (it doesn't), and that badgering, begging, or threatening an "okay" out of the objects of our desire is "good enough" consent (it isn't).

Unfortunately, the subcultures we create, refine, feel drawn to, or take refuge in often mirror many of these absurd values of the dominant culture. In the practice of good consent, we endeavour to better respect one another's boundaries, to become adept at asserting our own limits, and to embolden ourselves to fearlessly express our needs and desires in our sexual and romantic encounters so that our sex is as hot and passionate as it is safe and satisfying for all involved.

ANTICIPATING THE ENCOUNTER

When intimacy seems imminent, it is wise to discuss some vital issues beforehand which will not only make the rendezvous less awkward, but will make it more honest and accountable to everyone's needs and desires. Boundaries can be negotiated, safe words (words that mean "stop") can be agreed-upon, limits can be set, and past histories of surviving abuse or abusing others can be disclosed. It's imperative that those with STIs (sexually transmitted infections) disclose their positive STI status to whomever they might be putting at risk of catching said infection—to do otherwise is to violate the other person's informed consent. Which is to say, one's lovers might not have consented to sex had they known the inherent risk of the situation. Aside from the more stressful pre-coital conversations though, let us also imbue these moments with joy, by sharing our fantasies, kinks, erogenous areas, and how we most like to be pleasured with those who share our beds.

POWER AND PRIVILEGE

It's important to be aware of subtle or not-so-subtle power dynamics in one's relationships and trysts, as those undermine the ability of both parties to actively, enthusiastically, and equally consent to physical affection. In one's relationship, are there differentials in age, sexual experience, social status, cultural privilege, or sexual/BDSM role that make practicing good consent more challenging? Is there subtle pressure to "give in to" sex on either person's part, for fear of some sort of negative social, emotional, sexual, or physical consequence? Perhaps one lacks the confidence to say "no" and feels—or is made to feel—as though their rejection of their potential-lover is unreasonable, immature, or unfair. Deconstructing subtly coercive power dynamics relies heavily on careful introspection and good-faith communication.

WHEN A "YAY" BECOMES A "NAY"

Consent can be withdrawn at any time, for any reason. By definition, the refusal to cease performing physical, sexual, or BDSM-related acts on others after consent has been withdrawn is sexual assault. But how might one know (other than hearing a direct "no") that one's date, lover, partner, or submissive no longer desires certain acts being performed on them that they typically delight in, or to which they are seemingly consenting? Checking in verbally with one's partner(s) throughout the sexual encounter or BDSM scene and paying careful attention to body language are some wonderful ways to help keep things intentional and consensual, resulting in everyone involved feeling cared for, listened to, and safe. Good instances in which to check in are: when one is switching from touching one part of the body to another, in between performing a series of various sex acts, when those involved end up "going further" together than what was previously agreed upon, or when one might like to try out something completely new on or with their sweetheart. Some body language cues that might betray a lack of enthusiastic consent include: "freezing up," unresponsiveness, crying, looking away, squirming, or resisting in ways that are not a pre-agreed form of sexual play in the lovers' dynamic.

A CAUTIONARY NOTE ON SPIRITS

There are many differing opinions and nuances with regards to the consensual nature of sex induced by or following the mutual consumption of alcohol and drugs. Doubtless, alcohol and other mind-altering substances can cloud one's better judgment, lessen one's responsiveness, and confuse the senses, but what if all parties involved are about equally intoxicated? How much is "too much to consent," and what if you both would have consented to the encounter anyway, sober or not? These are complex and situational questions to consider, but generally speaking, imbibing intoxicating substances, no matter how smooth to the taste or delightful the initial sensory effect, does not create a situation conducive to practicing good consent, particularly when ingested in large quantities. Be mindful of your own sobriety and that of your sex partners, and whether there is a differential in your levels of intoxication. And it ought to be a given that someone who is passed out cannot consent to sex, whether lulled into slumber by the overindulgence of spirits or simply from fatigue.

When we put consent into practice in all aspects of our interpersonal relationships, we give ourselves and one another space to freely refuse that which we don't earnestly desire, and conversely, this makes a "yes" even more thrilling to hear uttered, for the is thus all the more genuine for it. Even the most light-hearted of trysts and outrageously decadent encounters require that we respect one another's boundaries, foster honest communication, and attempt to know our own selves deeply. And with this knowledge we can ask for, and often receive, all the transcendent pleasure and erotic connection our hearts and loins desire.

Many Loves:
AN INTRODUCTION TO POLYAMORY

O.M. Grey

POLYAMORY. MANY LOVES. THE TERM AND THE LIFESTYLE are gaining popularity, even in the mainstream, and it's no wonder. More people are choosing a non-monogamous lifestyle with each passing day. And who can blame them? With over 50% of marriages, 60% of second marriages, and 75% of third marriages ending in divorce, coupled with infidelity occurring in upwards of 85% of marriages, people are realizing that there must be a better way.

Monogamy and non-monogamy are both valid lifestyle choices; however, with a lifestyle like polyamory, there are no hard-and-fast rules. No one-size-fits-all, as is expected with a "traditional" relationship/marriage:

Find your one true love and live happily ever after.

> If they don't meet your every need every day
> forever and ever and ever and ever, some-
> thing is *wrong* with you, your partner, or
> your relationship.

Balderdash.

The basic concept behind polyamory, and other forms of ethical non-monogamy, is to establish and maintain multiple, loving, committed relationships.

- It is about being open and being honest, with yourself and your lovers.
- It is about facing your own insecurities.
- It is about being present and compassionate with your lovers' insecurities.
- It is about *a lot* of frank communication.
- It is about challenging fears.
- It is about taking responsibility for yourself and in your relationships.
- It is about maintaining integrity and finding courage in the face of "drama."
- It is about keeping yourself emotionally available.
- It is about talking about relationship issues as needed, as often as needed.
- It is about managing your time and your affections so that no one feels neglected.

What? It's not about a lot of great sex? It's not about or- gies and sex parties and doing what I want to whom I want whenever I want without accountability or responsibility? It's not about keeping all my options open in case some- one better comes along? It's not about fun and happiness and ecstasy all the time? It's not about avoiding drama and commitment?

Um, no.

It *is* about sex, lots and lots of great sex, if possible, but it is *also* about *love*. Lots and lots of beautiful love. And, contrary to what many think, it's about *deeper* commitment and *more* responsibility. If you think one relationship takes time and investment and effort, try three. A polyamorous lifestyle requires considerable amounts of integrity, self-awareness, courage, patience, and compassion, and the rewards are glorious:

Love breeds love.

Desire breeds desire.

In polyamorous relationships, each couple (or triad or quad, etc.) makes agreements that make sense to them and their relationship(s), which might be different than what works for another couple or triad or quad. Still, the foundation beneath all these agreements is honesty, responsibility, and integrity. Honesty with yourself and honesty with your partner(s).

Non-monogamy can span anywhere from very casual sex to deep meaningful relationships, and everything in between. Every non-monogamous lifestyle, as long as it's ethical, is perfectly fine in that sex-positive way, as long as everyone knows, everyone is on the same page, and everyone is respecting themselves and their lovers. This means taking care of your own heart and taking care of your lovers' hearts as well.

In the subculture of steampunk, many participants are identified as polyamorous or some other form of non-monogamy, like swinging or kinksters in the BDSM community. There is a lot of crossover between these communities. Steampunk has a large percentage of non-monogamous individuals, as well as other alternative lifestyles like BDSM and GLBT, because of the spirit from which the steampunk subculture emerged. We are the polite revolution. We hold manners and respect and integrity in high regard while rejecting commonly-held ideas in society that no longer serve us, nor society. We embrace the aesthetic of the distant past with more social awareness; forward thinking; and a DIY mentality, without buying into what society dictates. From costuming and gadgetry, to modding and relationship styles, steampunks do it themselves, and they do it with well-lubricated gears.

As with any matters of the heart and soul, romance and sexuality contain fears, insecurities, and "drama." These things just don't disappear when one identifies as polyamorous. In fact, if anything, they multiply. More relationships equal more effort. More time. More investment. More talking and talking and talking. More responsibility.

With all that also comes more fun and more love and *more sex!*

In good conscience, I must give a warning to those wanting to open their lives to polyamory or another form of ethical non-monogamy. Beware of the mad scientist type and emotional vampires. Just like those I write about in my fiction, I have found that open, honest lifestyles which revolve around sex-positivity create a feeding frenzy for sexual and emotional predators. So please be careful. Take things slow, talk to others in your community, share your experiences, and don't let that vampire feed off you or your loved one.

Make no mistake. Polyamory, although fun and loving and wondrous and sexy, is not all fun and games. Another person's heart and body and mind and soul are not toys with which to be played. Remember that.

Respect yourself.

Respect your lovers.

Love openly and honestly.
Have a euphoric, sexy time.

More information on polyamory, other forms of non-monogamy, and dealing with relationship issues:

- Loving More. LOVEMORE.COM
- *The Ethical Slut.* Celestial Arts. 2009.
- *Sex at Dawn.* Harper Perennial. 2011.
- *Opening Up.* Cleis Press. 2008.
- *The Art and Etiquette of Polyamory.* Skyhorse Publishing. 2011.
- Caught in the Cogs. OMGREY.WORDPRES.COM
- Successful Non-monogamy. SUCCESSFULNONMONOGAMY.COM/V1
- Open Fidelity. OPENFIDELITY.INFO

Creepers:
HOW TO DEAL WITH, AND NOT BE, A CREEP

KC Crowell

CONVENTIONS ARE FANTASTIC PLACES—THEY OFFER THE chance for steampunk enthusiasts, artists, musicians, tinkers, and troublemakers to come together in the pursuit of advancing awesomeness. Oh, the things you will see! Oh, the people you will meet! Unfortunately, sometimes people get a little too caught up in the moment at conventions, which can lead to the emergence of a most unfortunate kind of person: The Creep.

"Creep" is a catch-all term for a person who, intentionally or not, makes you feel uncomfortable or violates your personal boundaries. Creepy behavior can be anything from unwelcome touching to unsolicited sexual comments. Creeps might be well meaning, or they might also have more sinister ulterior motives. Regardless, here are some handy tips to those who may find themselves in the path of a Creep, along with some tips for those of you who wish to never be burdened with the label of Creep.

WHAT TO DO WHEN APPROACHED BY A CREEP

1. DISENGAGE. When approached by a Creep, the easiest way to avoid contact is to simply smile and excuse yourself. You should feel no expectation to endorse someone's bad behavior with your company. Of course, this is of little use if you are interested in correcting the Creep's behavior, or if they choose to pursue you. If that is the case...

2. ...ENGAGE! There are a few simple phrases that can be used to engage and diffuse creepy behavior. "Please do not touch me," or "I do not feel comfortable with this conversation" can serve as handy verbal stop signs for unwelcome attention. If they don't work the first time, firmly repeat them until the desired effect is achieved.

3. CONTACT A STAFF MEMBER. Convention staff are there to facilitate your positive experience, not harbor creepy or abusive attendees. If there is someone bothering you, bring it to the attention of a convention organizer. They may not have all the power to immediately fix the issue or remove the offender, but making creepy behavior visible is an important step to curbing future offenders.

HOW NOT TO BE A CREEP

1. NEVER, EVER ASSUME THAT CONVENTION ATTEND-EES ARE THERE FOR YOUR PERSONAL ENTERTAIN-MENT OR BENEFIT. That dapperly-dressed gentleman? That lovely lady in a tight corset and short skirt? They are wearing those things because it makes them feel fantastic, not because they are looking to be ogled, groped, or propositioned by strangers.

2. ALWAYS ASK PERMISSION. A compliment or caress might make someone feel admired. However, a quick "may I compliment you?" or "may I kiss your hand?" will make them feel respected, valued, and like their consent is taken seriously.

3. GET CALLED OUT AS A CREEPER? Don't flip out. Everyone makes mistakes. Getting called a creeper is not the end of the world, and the worst thing to do in this situation is to dig yourself deeper by loudly proclaiming that you did not do anything creepy, or worse, that the accusing party was somehow "asking for" unwanted attention. Never underestimate the power of a humble apology over righteous indignation.

Cupid's Table: APHRODISIACS

Professor Calamity

IN MRS. MEYERS' INFLUENTIAL 1856 LADIES MANUAL, SHE warns women: "never serve from Cupid's table unless you are safely married and your husband will be home for the evening." So just what food and drink might scoundrels use to arouse the mood?

UNPREPARED FOODS

ASPARAGUS was served to 19th century bridegrooms to ensure they would be properly aroused for their wedding night. They would munch on the phallic vegetable for breakfast, lunch, and dinner on the day of their marriage.

BANANAS were considered a very saucy wedding gift to present to a bride not only due to their shape, but also due to their creamy, lush texture. Further, some studies suggest that the enzyme bromelain found in bananas enhances male performance.

CAVIAR became associated with sexuality in the West during the mid-19th century and was served in dancing saloons as far from the sea as Topeka, Kansas. Caviar is high in zinc, which stimulates the formation of testosterone, maintaining male functionality.

CHAMPAGNE, not surprisingly, was considered the "drink of love" in the 19th century. It still continues to be associated with romance. Studies show alcohol in all of it varieties reduces anxiety and lowers inhibitions—bars have been making money on that formula for ages.

CHOCOLATE, usually melted and served as a drink, was served in US bordellos during the Victorian times and "hot chocolate" was actually slang for prostitute in the US and Canada. Chocolate contains both a sedative, which relaxes and lowers inhibitions, and a stimulant that increases activity and the desire for physical contact.

OYSTERS are another 19th century aphrodisiac that are still being used as such today. In the Victorian period, zoologists discovered that some oysters repeatedly change their sex from male to female and back, giving rise to claims that the oyster lets one experience both the masculine and feminine sides of love.

NIGHT STRAWBERRIES

Night strawberries combined cream cheese (a new concoction in Victorian times) with two foods long considered aphrodisiacs: strawberries and melted chocolate.

Ingredients
- 20 fresh strawberries
- 1 (3 ounce) package cream cheese, softened
- 2 tablespoons chopped walnuts
- 1 ½ tablespoons confectioners' sugar

Directions
1. Dice two strawberries and set aside. Cut the stems off of each of the remaining strawberries, forming a base for strawberries to stand on. Starting at the pointed ends and cutting most of the way, but not completely through, the stem end, slice each strawberry into four wedges.
2. Beat the cream cheese until fluffy; stir in the diced strawberries, walnuts, and powdered sugar. Spoon or pipe about a teaspoon of mix into each strawberry.

ARROWS OF PASSION

This was a favorite of Boss Tweed, a 19th century machine-boss of New York. He wrote a letter to his lovelorn friend, Governor Charles Murphy, and included this recipe along with a lewd drawing.

Ingredients
- 1 pound fresh asparagus spears, trimmed
- 1 (8 ounce) container yogurt

- 1 handful of raspberries
- ½ lemon, juiced

Directions

1. Place the asparagus in a steamer basket and set over about 1 inch of boiling water. Cover, then steam for 5 to 8 minutes or until tender and bright green.
2. In a small saucepan, stir together the yogurt, crushed raspberries, and lemon juice. Cook over medium heat until warmed.
3. Place steamed asparagus onto serving plates and spoon the sauce over, or serve sauce separately.

DOUX AMOUR

This name of this appetizer means "sweet love" in French. It mixes a number foods—all considered powerful sexual stimulants at the time—in a single torte.

Ingredients:

- 1 cup finely chopped red onion
- 1 cup champagne
- 2 (8 ounce) packages cream cheese, whipped
- 16 eggs, hard-cooked, coarsely chopped
- ½ cup mayonnaise
- 1 teaspoon salt
- ½ teaspoon white pepper
- ½ clove garlic, minced
- 2 teaspoons fresh lemon juice
- ½ ounce black caviar
- water crackers

Preparation:

1. Place the red onions and champagne in a large skillet over medium-high heat. Cook until the champagne reduces completely, 10 minutes.

2. Remove from heat and stir into the cream cheese. Cover and set aside.

3. In another bowl, mix together the hard-boiled eggs and mayonnaise. Season with $\frac{1}{2}$ teaspoon of salt and $\frac{1}{4}$ teaspoon of the pepper and mix. Cover and set aside.

4. In another bowl, mix together the garlic and lemon juice. Season with the remaining $\frac{1}{2}$ teaspoon salt and $\frac{1}{4}$ teaspoon pepper, and mix.

5. Layer ingredients in a 10" springform pan. Spread the egg mixture on the bottom and smooth the top until even. Spread the other mixtures on top of the egg mixture and smooth the top until even. Spread the cream cheese mixture on top of the avocado mixture and smooth the top until even.

6. Cover with plastic wrap and chill at least 3 hours or until firm. (Torte can be made up to 2 days in advance.)

7. Just before serving, spread an even layer of caviar on top of torte.

8. Place flowers or a thin lemon slice in the center of the torte. Set crackers around the base.

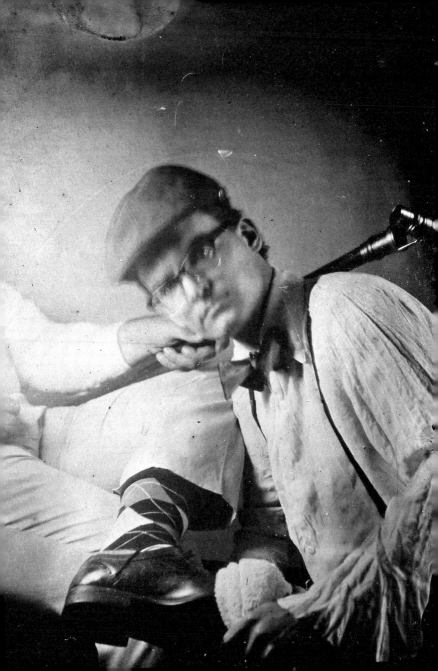

Acknowledgements

This book would not be possible without the help of those who backed us on Kickstarter, the models who appear in these pages, and so many others. In particular we'd like to thank:

Campbell Allan
The Artifice Club
Dan Barbulescu
bayleaf
Ben
Shaun Bensinger
Simon Berman
Michael Beverland
bht
Willow Bl00
Bluechapel
Bluesolis
Christoph Boget
Allen Bonin
Max Bowes
Kathleen Bradean
Don J Brancaccio
Buddha Buck
Mr. Robert Buktenica
Libby Bulloff
H. N. Bur
Chris J. Burris
Travis Carpenter
Cherie
Deb Clark
J. Cunningham
Christa B. Daring
Olivier Davenport
Davenport & Winkleperry
Darren Davis

Jessie Dawn
Cory Doctorow
Rebecca Dominguez
Nate Doty
Octavian Düm
Robert Dunn (roopot)
Lara Eckener
Vincent Ecuyer
Patricia Eddy
Mikela Farley
Mark Farrelly
Sean J Faul
Robert Fernandez
Michelle "Lady Kaieta" Flamm
Michelle Fleming
Red. Florian
Chelsea Flowers
Ann Forseth
Daniel Garcia
Micah "Tried to Troll Me" Gates
Mister and Madame Geleynse
gerG
Shanna Germain
Rich Gibson
Giles Corey Press
Lyra Goldman
Clitomus Gordon, Steampunk Adult Toys
Gorpli
O. M. Grey
SmittyHalibut

Harry Halpin
Brigitte & Walter Hammerschmid
Benjamin Hendy
Harald
Hasher
Sascha "derTourist" von Hoff
Edward Iglesias
Glen Ivey
Jim "mayotta"
Jessi
Meinos Kaen
Regina Kammer
Kate Khatib
Joshua Knox & Danielle Roberts
Martin L
H.O. Laertes
Michael S Lang
Myrrh Larsen
Payne Lawler
Jeff Lewis
Lpff
Kyle A. Lovett
lucha
Colly Lustre
Liam Jensz
Loren K
Magda Kamenev
Andrew Kelly
D. L. King
Sarah E. B. H. Kiniry

Baron Von Krakenhunter
Vladimir Kuznetsov
Dr. L
Jacob Larimore
Miss Lily
Bryce A. Lynch
Kristan Mackintosh
Madrone
Bergen R. McMurray
Kevin McNally
The Mediocre Pumpkin Lady
MegaZone
Valerie L. Meiss
Hon. T.C. Merriweather
Lauren & Michal Minecki
Mick
Robbo Mills
MLH
Shean 'Momo' Mohammed
Sarah Kathryn Moore
Jaden Munoz
Rupert H. Murgatroyd
Ron Neely II
Chris Newell
Ani Niow
LithicSpiral S. K. Nord
noxturne
Alaina and James O'Carra
Oliver Ockenden
Bob Ohm

Lindsay Oliver
Lady Overkill
Maria Padilla
Kelsey Paul
Tom "The Buhda" Peterson III
Verane Pick, Counter Intelligence
Media
Le Pief
PK
Cheryl Preyer
Prometheus & Savageseas
PUSH Festish Event
MLE Raiford
Shai Ravid
Bill Raymond
Lisa Reddig
reginazabo
Beth Rimmels
Jordan Ritter
Robin
S. M. Robinson
j. rochkind
Laurie Rockenbeck
E. Romson
Josh Rose
Karen and Tom Rosencek
Ryan and Ari
Catherine S.
Martin Sattler
Michael P. Sauers
Greg Schilling
SeanK
Sed the Cursed
Suzanne Shaffer
Jim Sheppard

Yann SICAMOIS
Jon Brede Skaug
Skyman
Brett Slocum
Smashingsuns
Steampunk Revue
Chris Stankaitis
Thomas "Tie-fighter" Steinbrenner
Kieran Stones
Ulrich Strasser
Janne Syrjakoski
Doctor Q
H. Taylor
Kody Tench
Techknight Tenente
Carl Tipple
Jeremy & Kristina Treadwell
Professor Upsidasium
Julien V.
Vernian Process
Chad & Kim Wagner
Eric Wagoner
Frances Watson
Rachel & Simon Waugh
Thomas Willeford
Kira Williams
Michael Willis
Doug Wilson
John R. Withee
David Witteven
Paul Woolman
Wyng'd Lyon Creations
Scott Wooldridge
TheXenocide
Igor Zusev

ABOUT COMBUSTION BOOKS

Combustion books is a collectively-run publisher of dangerous fiction. We specialize in genre stories that confront, subvert, or rudely ignore the dominant paradigm and we're not afraid to get our hands dirty or our houses raided by the government. How many fiction publishers can promise you that?

Rejecting the dominant paradigm doesn't end with the stories we tell. We operate without bosses and we pay ourselves and our authors outright for work in order to keep us from getting mired in the world of profit-driven publishing.

One of our goals is to break down the hierarchy of the publishing world and develop relationships with our authors and audience that go beyond those offered by a traditional press.

We're open to manuscript submissions and delight in working with new and un-agented authors. We are primarily interested in novel-length (40,000+ words) genre fiction of a radical bent. Genres we're seeking include SF, Fantasy, Horror, Steampunk, Mystery, and New Weird.

Please attach completed manuscripts for consideration, in .rtf, .doc, .odt, or .docx format, to an email directed to SUBMISSIONS@COMBUSTIONBOOKS.ORG. We will respond within 30 days of receiving your submission. Please do not send multiple manuscripts: send only your best work. If you have written a series, send only the first in the series.

WWW.COMBUSTIONBOOKS.ORG